ON

DENNETT

John Symons
Boston University

WADSWORTH

THOMSON LEARNING

Australia • Canada • Mexico • Singapore • Spain
United Kingdom • United States

WADSWORTH

™

THOMSON LEARNING

Printed in the United States of America
1 2 3 4 5 6 7 04 03 02 01 00

For permission to use material from this text, contact us:
Web: http://www.thomsonrights.com
Fax: 1-800-730-2215
Phone: 1-800-730-2214

For more information, contact:
Wadsworth/Thomson Learning, Inc.
10 Davis Drive
Belmont, CA 94002-3098
USA
http://www.wadsworth.com

ISBN: 0-534-57632-X

Contents

Preface

This book is a self-contained, general and non-technical introduction to the work of the American philosopher Daniel Dennett. From his positions as Distinguished Arts and Sciences Professor, Professor of Philosophy, and Director of the Center for Cognitive Studies at Tufts University, Dennett has become one of the most prominent figures in both philosophy and cognitive science. His ability to integrate philosophical and scientific investigations of mental life has set the tone and direction for contemporary philosophy of mind and has had a significant impact on the brain and behavioral sciences. Marvin Minsky, one of the pioneering figures in artificial intelligence, has called Dennett "our best current philosopher... Unlike traditional philosophers, Dan is a student of neuroscience, linguistics, artificial intelligence, computer science, and psychology. He's redefining and reforming the role of the philosopher."[1]

The interplay between science and philosophy forms the central theme of this book. The best way to understand the virtues of this interplay is to examine its effect on specific philosophical problems. In the pages that follow I focus on consciousness and intentionality. The notions of intentionality and consciousness were once exclusively the business of philosophers rather than scientists. Focusing on these traditionally philosophical notions is intended to demonstrate how Dennett's openness to natural science has transformed philosophy. His way of asking questions about the mind has challenged traditional philosophical dogma and has led to a fundamental rethinking of the relationship between mental life and the natural world.

I have tried very hard to convey the radicalism and optimism of Dennett's philosophy to the general reader or student who has little training in philosophy. Hence, at the risk of boring more seasoned

---

[1] *Edge Magazine* (http://www.edge.org/3rd_culture/bios/dennett.html)

readers I spend some time in the early chapters introducing and explaining the central problems in the philosophy of mind. At any rate, I am confident that philosophers interested in understanding Dennett's views will also find it useful to reconsider some of the historical, philosophical and scientific background to his work.

ACKNOWLEDGMENTS

This book derives from lectures I gave in my course on Minds and Machines at Emerson College in Boston in the Fall of 1999. I want to acknowledge the help given to me by the students and staff of Emerson's Institute for Interdisciplinary Studies and the Liberal Arts. This book was greatly improved by discussions with many people over the past few years, including the patient and encouraging Dan Kolak, as well as readers and editors at Wadsworth. I am very grateful to my friends, teachers and colleagues, with special thanks to John Bickle, Tian Yu Cao, Troy Catterson, Jaakko Hintikka, Juliet Floyd, Aaron Garrett, Stefan Kalt, Marie Taylor, and Charles Wolfe. Finally, I would also like to thank Dan Dennett for his helpful comments on a penultimate draft of this book.

John Symons

Abbreviations

References to Dennett's works are given in the text by the following abbreviations:

BBS   'Précis of *The Intentional Stance*' in *Brain and Behavioral Sciences* (1988) **11**, 495-546

BC   *Brainchildren: Essays on Designing Minds*. Cambridge, Mass.: MIT Press, A Bradford Book, 1998.

BR   *Brainstorms: Philosophical Essays on Mind and Psychology*. Montgomery, Vt.: Bradford Books, 1978.

CC   *Content and Consciousness*. International Library of Philosophy and Scientific Method. New York: Humanities Press; London: Routledge & Kegan Paul, 1969.

CE   *Consciousness Explained*. Boston: Little, Brown, 1991.

DDI   *Darwin's Dangerous Idea: Evolution and the Meanings of Life*. New York: Simon and Schuster; London: Allen Lane, 1995.

ER   *Elbow Room: The Varieties of Free Will Worth Wanting*. Cambridge, Mass.: MIT Press, 1984.

IS   *The Intentional Stance*. Cambridge, Mass.: MIT Press, 1987.

KM   *Kinds of Minds: Toward an Understanding of Consciousness*. (The Science Masters Series.) New York: Basic Books, 1996.

I also use the following abbreviations for other works cited frequently

WO   Quine, W.V.O. *Word and Object*, Cambridge, MA: MIT Press, 1960.

COM   Ryle, G. *The Concept of Mind*, London: Hutchinson's, 1949.

DAC   Dahlbom, B. (ed.) *Dennett and his Critics*, Oxford: Blackwell, 1993.

1

Introducing Dennett

Daniel Dennett has been one of the most important voices in the philosophical and scientific discussions of the mind for the past thirty years. While many other philosophers see the mind as a mystery that will never succumb to explanation, Dennett's work opens the door to scientific inquiry, showing ways to understand difficult phenomena like perception, the will and consciousness using the techniques of ordinary scientific investigation. Philosophers have long debated whether science is powerful enough to explain the place of mental life in the natural world. Dennett's work offers hope to the optimists and poses a serious challenge to the lovers of mystery. Unlike many prominent philosophers in the second half of the twentieth century, he has always embraced scientific inquiry enthusiastically.

As we shall see, Dennett's work shows how to connect the scientific investigation of the body with the commonsense descriptions of mental life that form an indispensable part of ordinary experience. There is still considerable debate over his approach to the mind and his views have undergone some changes over the years in response to his critics. Furthermore, Dennett is likely to remain an extremely energetic and important force in philosophy for many years to come. Therefore it's far too early to pass any final judgment on his philosophical work as a whole. Nevertheless it is already clear that Dennett has responded to traditional philosophical mysteries by offering an important new way for us to think about some very old problems.

Dennett's Perspective

Traditionally, philosophers have offered theories about the nature of mind, its parts, its relationship to the *external world* and most famously, of course, its relationship to the body. While Dennett's philosophy certainly sheds light on these issues, it does so from a rather unorthodox perspective.

The most distinctive aspect of Dennett's approach to the mind is his choice of starting point. Rather than diving immediately into traditional questions about the nature of mental entities, he begins by investigating what we ordinarily say or write about other minds. Conversation or language, Dennett writes, is the royal road to the knowledge of other minds. (KM, 13) So, rather than immediately focusing on the *terra incognita* of what the mind actually is, he focuses instead on the practical role played by the terms we use to talk about the mind, terms like 'belief', 'desire', 'the will', 'consciousness' etc. Dennett's interest lies in understanding the ordinary commonsense descriptions of other minds that we find so useful in our daily lives. What are we doing, for instance, when we say that another person believes, desires or imagines something? And why does our talk of what people think, want, or hope, seem to work so well in ordinary life?

Most philosophers of mind have tended to focus on the nature of 'belief' itself rather than the process of interpretation by which we come to know the beliefs of another person or animal. Generally, researchers begin with the assumption that words like 'belief', desire' and the like refer to mental entities of some kind. For the most part, philosophers were not overly concerned with the ways we come to know those mental entities, since presumably, even if we encounter some difficulty when it comes to other minds, our own minds are easy enough to examine. Dennett does not assume that these mental entities exist. Instead, his approach is to remain agnostic (at least initially) towards the meaning of psychological terms like 'belief', 'desire', etc. Rather than assuming that the word 'belief' refers to some kind of entity in the mind or brain, he focuses instead on the role such terms play in practice. In effect, this means that he begins by considering the reasons we use words like 'belief' and 'desire' rather than the nature of belief and desire *per se*. By focusing on what we do when we interpret or describe the mental life of another person or animal, Dennett redirects our attention from traditional philosophical puzzles and opens fertile new lines of inquiry for both scientists and philosophers.

This subtle shift in perspective changes the contour of philosophical problems considerably. Instead of worrying about the mysterious inner workings of other minds, or the problem of how the mind and body interact, we look instead to the publicly observable utterances we use to describe one another. These utterances, along with the contexts in which they appear, form an objective starting point for a more scientific approach to the problems posed by mental life. In principle, it should be possible to study the relationship between these patterns of utterances and the underlying processes that take place in the brain and central nervous system.

According to Dennett, our use of psychological terms arises primarily out of our interest in predicting the behavior of people and other animals. For obvious reasons, animals need a way to anticipate the behavior of possible mates, predators, prey and competition. This is accomplished in a variety of ways in different species. Naturally, we humans are most familiar with the techniques employed by mammals like ourselves. While mammals have an array of techniques for predicting behavior, humans tend to be especially biased towards visual cues of various kinds. By watching the eyes, posture and motion of other mammals we can generally predict their behavior into the very near future with some accuracy. So, how do we manage these remarkable prophecies? Is it a matter of knowing the mind of the other person or animal?

For Dennett, Darwin's theory of evolution through natural selection provides the key to understanding our amazing ability to predict the behavior of other animals. Over the course of natural history, those who fail to reliably anticipate the future behavior of relevant others soon perish. As a result, a significant number of species have evolved to become masters in the art of predicting the futures of massively complex biological systems. For example, without knowing anything about the physiological processes taking place under the animal's skin or in its mind, most of us can predict, with relative certainty, what a hungry dog is likely to do when we offer it a bowl of food. Our ability to predict the behavior of other biological systems is not the result of an ability to somehow see inside the minds of other animals. Instead, according to Dennett, our interpretations are the product of a skill that has been sculpted by a long process of natural selection. Our ability to accurately predict the future behavior of other creatures based on the evidence of their past behavior is a skill that we, along with many other animals, simply inherited.

So, for example, few of us understand that when we gaze into the eyes of our beloved, we are subtly monitoring the degree to which his or her pupils are dilated. Our pupils automatically dilate when we like what we see, and since we like people who like us, we regularly monitor the pupils of our potential lovers. We have evolved sensitivity to countless biological cues of this kind. Advertisers who artificially enlarge the pupils on the smiling faces in their adverts, as well as the renaissance ladies who dropped belladonna in their eyes to achieve similar effects, have long been aware of this particular principle.

However, unlike other animals, we humans have the added advantage of a rich symbolic language with which to articulate and share our predictive strategies. Language has opened expansive new vistas for human life. It provides a far more flexible way of preserving the winning strategies of past generations than one that relies solely on shaping behavior through genetic inheritance. And it allows us access to a kind of virtual world filled with useful and interesting abstractions. With language, we are not completely tethered to the immediate reality of our circumstances and instead we can use the virtual tools that our cultural inheritance provides to consider a range of alternative scenarios and possibilities.

With the ability to speak and write we develop theories about the patterns we see in animal and human behavior. Our ordinary way of talking about the behavior of a hungry pet dog, for example might go something like this:

(1) Rex wants to eat.
(2) He believes that there is food in his bowl.
(3) Unless there is something wrong with the dog (or the food), this belief (2) combined with his desire for food (1) will cause him to eat.

The patterns of belief, desire and action that we recognize in the behavior of others obviously serve as an indispensable aid to our survival and flourishing. As we have seen, Dennett's approach is to begin with the biological necessities that shape the strategies we adopt to cope with the behavior of other animals. These strategies are built around the observation that certain patterns of behavior repeat. With the addition of a complex symbolic language we humans can represent these patterns to ourselves and manipulate them in a variety of useful ways. In 'Three Kinds of Intentional Psychology' (1981) Dennett introduced the term *folk psychology* to describe our use of these patterns. Many philosophers have seen folk psychology as a kind of proto-scientific theory; a theory that makes claims about minds in the same way physics makes claims about the solar system or the constituents of the atom.

Philosophers who take this kind of position have long worried about the nature of the things that folk psychology talks about. What are beliefs, desires and thoughts? Does everyone have them? How can we know what other people are really thinking or feeling? Can machines think? Can aardvarks? Our ordinary picture of the mind, when it is made explicit and compared with the kinds of theories that we see in the physical sciences, gives rise to these and other problems. For centuries, philosophers have puzzled over our ability to know other minds, the mechanisms that underlie thought and consciousness and, of course, the relationship between mental life and the physical world.

Such questions and problems are put in a very different light once we shift our perspective in the way that Dennett's philosophy suggests. According to Dennett, we should begin by recognizing that it takes at least two animals in an ecological setting where behavior must be reliably anticipated before we can even begin talking about mental life. Rather than beginning with the assumption that we have access to some kind of inner mental life, Dennett starts from the outside. Whereas traditional philosophers and psychologists have treated our ordinary talk of beliefs and desires as a kind of proto-scientific theory about the contents of a private inner world, Dennett focuses on the practical role played by those terms from the perspective of the objective observer. As he shows throughout his writings, the virtual world of belief and desire only emerges once animals are in the business of predicting and interpreting one another.

While some philosophers have tended to see our ordinary talk of mental life as constituting a primitive kind of scientific theory, as Dennett points out, the social and contextual nature of our view of mental life means that it differs significantly from the knowledge we gleam from the physical sciences. Our ordinary beliefs about mental life arise in a linguistic, social and philosophical context that differs significantly from the theories of less obviously interpersonal sciences. And while there must be some social component to all science, Dennett reminds us that folk psychology differs fundamentally from physics. While physics claims to talk about things that exist independently of the interpreter, folk psychology is always tangled up in the interests and context of the observer.

The physicist and the folk psychologist adopt very different approaches to the objects they study. Dennett has characterized these approaches as distinct interpretive stances. (See Chapter Four) The *physical stance* provides a description of what Dennett calls "the actual physical state of the particular object... [it is] ...worked out by applying whatever knowledge we have of the laws of nature. It is from this stance alone that we can predict the malfunction of a system." (BR,4) Basically, according to Dennett, the physical stance is the approach that physicists (in their professional lives) take towards the world. By contrast, we folk psychologists adopt what Dennett calls *the intentional stance* towards other creatures. Very briefly, the intentional stance is the strategy of prediction and explanation that attributes beliefs, desires and other "intentional" states to systems.

For Dennett, when we say that an animal, a person or an artifact believes, desires or thinks something, our statement should be understood as if it was part of an attempt to predict or to control the behavior of the organism or machine that we are talking about. The attempt to predict or control the behavior of another animal is always influenced by the interests of the animal or person who is doing the controlling and predicting. So while the physicists can talk about planets and electrons as objects existing independently of their interests and apart from the linguistic and social context of the researcher (at least to a certain extent). This is not so clearly the case when we talk about, for example, beliefs.

The idea behind the intentional stance is that an observer can predict the behavior of an organism from what the observer calculates it would be rational for that organism or machine to do. The idea of rationality here simply amounts to the assumption that the animal or machine wants what's good for it and that it's aware of the relevant aspects of its environment. With the right "beliefs" and the right "desires" in place, a rational system will pursue a course of action that helps it achieve its ends. An observer can anticipate what this course of action will be and can therefore predict the future behavior of the organism and machine with reasonable confidence. Chapter Four will present a detailed discussion of the intentional stance and will examine a number of important criticisms that it faces.

Darwin's theory of evolution through natural selection is the cornerstone of modern biology and it plays a central role in Dennett's philosophy. The intentional stance is useful simply because animals who respond inappropriately to their environment, as well as animals desiring things that are bad for them, soon leave the biological stage. Thus, after many generations of selection, it is a pretty good bet that most of the animals we encounter will comply with the principle of rationality, i.e., they want what's good for them and they respond appropriately to their immediate environment. There are, of course, exceptions. However, human and animal behavior is guided by the way things ordinarily are and tends to discount occasional exceptions from the rule.

Are Minds Real?

Beyond Dennett's application of Darwinism to the philosophy of mind, perhaps the most important philosophical contribution of Dennett's theory is its emphasis on the role of the interpreter in the ascription of beliefs and desires to the system in question. According to Dennett, ascribing a 'belief' or a 'desire' to some system is not the same as describing some portion of the physical world. Instead, according to Dennett it's more like performing a mathematical calculation.

For Dennett, beliefs and desires are like centers of gravity, equators or lines of force – they are virtual tools that allow us to simplify the behavior of otherwise massively complex systems. For example, an astronomer might, for the sake of simplicity, treat the motion of a planet in terms of the motion of a single point, a center of gravity. The astronomer would almost certainly agree that the center of gravity isn't *really* hidden deep in the planet's core. He or she would tell us that the center of gravity is a theoretical device that allows us to conveniently track gravitational systems with the minimum of extraneous calculation. In a sense, the center of gravity is something that exists only in the calculations of the astronomer. This is the case even though the predictions that the astronomers calculations provide might be extremely accurate. It's not that Dennett is denying the objectivity of statements about belief, rather he is committed to denying that beliefs, desires and other intentional entities exist in the same way that the entities of the physical science exist.

This way of thinking about beliefs and desires happens to be extremely radical. Many philosophers have understood Dennett's position to mean that mental life doesn't really exist, and that folk psychology is just an illusion. It has been difficult to avoid charges that Dennett has made the mind something that is *merely* in the eye of the beholder. This charge is associated with the labels *interpretationist, relativist* and *instrumentalist.* Many philosophers have argued that Dennett's instrumentalist position with respect to the mind makes little or no sense since it denies the reality of something we know with the utmost certainty. It seems insane to deny that we really have beliefs. Similarly, it makes little sense to say that the only reason you or I have beliefs or desires is because some third person interprets us as having them. If it were solely a matter of interpretation, then that third person would himself be an interpreter only in the eyes of some fourth interpreter, who would in turn be an interpreter in the eyes of some fifth interpreter, and so on into an infinite regress. Arguments such as these have convinced many philosophers that Dennett must be wrong.

However, Dennett is not denying the truth of statements about belief. For example, it is true that as I write these words, alone at my desk, I believe my coffee is cold. This is true, despite the fact that there is nobody here to interpret my behavior. In an effort to clarify his position, Dennett's 1991 article, 'Real Patterns' Dennett reminds us that the virtual objects he describes, like centers of gravity and planetary equators are more than mere arbitrary interpretations of reality. They allow us to understand and predict *real patterns* of behavior. Ultimately, Dennett believes that the truth of an ascription of belief or desire to another biological or mechanical system is determined by whether taking a certain interpretive stance would allow one to generate accurate predictions. Dennett summarizes his attitude towards the existence of beliefs as follows:

> My thesis is that while belief is a perfectly objective phenomenon (which apparently makes me a realist), it can be discerned only from the point of view of someone who adopts a certain predictive strategy, *the intentional stance* (which apparently makes me an interpretationist). (BBS 496)

In Chapter Four we will examine Dennett's views on the reality of belief in considerable detail. As I hope to demonstrate, Dennett's account of the intentional stance solves more problems than it generates and offers an elegant and productive way for us to think about the mind.

Dennett's work has had consequences far beyond its immediate effect on the philosophy and science of mind. He has played a central role in changing the way we understand the nature of philosophical problems, the nature of philosophy and the relationship between philosophy and natural science.

Dennett's ability to integrate philosophy, psychology and the study of artificial intelligence has set the tone and direction for contemporary philosophy of mind. Even philosophers who explicitly disagree with Dennett's characterization of the mind now follow him in acknowledging the role of empirical research in the solution of traditional philosophical problems. It is often said that Dennett, more than any other philosopher, has made his colleagues recognize the relevance of empirical studies to the practice of philosophy. Perhaps more remarkable than his effect on philosophers has been Dennett's ability to make psychologists and other natural scientists appreciate the role of philosophical analysis in the development of scientific theories. (See for example Yu and Fuller (1986)) His work exemplifies and has encouraged the growing interplay between science and philosophy.

The most exciting intellectual challenge facing philosophy and science in our time is to understand the place of mental life in the physical world. In recent decades, imaging technologies have allowed neuroscientists new windows into the activity and structure of the brain. These non-invasive imaging technologies along with improved methods of surgical and genetic manipulation of the nervous system and the massive computational power that neuroscientists now have at their fingertips have led to dramatic new contributions to human self-knowledge. We are now able to treat knowledge and experience as an object of scientific inquiry in ways unparalleled in history. However, there are enormous conceptual gaps between the way we ordinarily think of ourselves and the picture of human life that natural science presents. The next section briefly examines some of the recent discussion surrounding the gap between scientific knowledge and our view of the mind.

A Brief History of Recent Philosophy of Mind

In the twentieth century, many philosophers have offered ways to understand the place of mental life in the physical world. For example, one common solution in the 1960's was to insist that psychological and physical terms both referred to the same thing. This view, which came to be known as the identity theory claimed that neuroscience would allow us to understand how neurophysiological structures and processes were responsible for what we think of as mental life. The idea was that we could, for example, some day prove that pain *is* the firing of C-fibers. Mind and brain are contingently identical according to philosophers like U.T. Place. Place was one of the first thinkers in contemporary philosophy of mind to defend the hypothesis that consciousness itself was simply a brain state. (1956) If Place is right, then for each theoretical statement that appears in psychology, (P) there must be a true statement that articulates a psychophysical identity. (P=N) Where 'N' is a neural state, 'P' is a theoretical statement of psychology and 'P=N' is a psychophysical identity statement. These are called contingent identity statements because they could have been

9

otherwise. For example, instead of P=N it might have been the case that P=D; that psychological states were identical with digestive states.

The identity theory was widely criticized in the sixties and seventies for its failure to account for the multiple realizability of mental phenomena. Something is multiply realizable if it can be supported by a variety of different mechanisms. For example we would say that pain is multiply realizable if we agreed that cuttlefish, who have no C-fibers can feel pain. If we agree that pain can occur in animals that do not have C-fibers then it is false to assert that the concept pain and the concept C-fiber really refer to the same thing. This criticism of the identity theory provided a central point of agreement in the philosophy of mind from the late sixties until very recently.

Like most contemporary philosophers, Dennett has been a critic of the identity theory. However, in his first book *Content and Consciousness* Dennett's analysis took a different tack from the usual criticisms of the identity theory. In his early work, Dennett recognized the appeal of the identity theory as a means of retaining an allegiance to natural science and the meaningfulness of psychological terms. (CC, 4) However, Dennett questions the identity theory's basic assumption – the idea that if words refer, then they must refer to everything in the same way. While the identity theorist assumes that things cannot exist in different ways, the alternative that Dennett presents throughout his work takes a more flexible position with respect to the kinds of things that can be said to exist. For Dennett we can talk about the existence of chairs, tables, cabbages and kings, but we can also talk about the existence of numbers, sets, centers of gravity, opportunities, deficits and dints.

For Dennett, nouns in true sentences do not all refer in the same way. Like the ordinary language philosophers Ludwig Wittgenstein, John Austin and Gilbert Ryle, Dennett has been extremely sensitive to the different ways language can be used. And yet, Dennett recognized that while it might be correct to allow sentences about the existence of opportunities, minds, dints and the like to be called true, liberalism with respect to the various meanings of 'exist' will not, by itself, provide the basis for a solution to the scientific problem of mind. The problem remains as to how scientists can legitimately include psychological entities in their picture of the natural world.

In the 1960's the digital computer seemed to provide a way to explain how mental life could be embodied. Computational functionalists, inspired by the relatively new technology, saw a way to understand how we could individuate (pick out) mental states without referring to mental entities that differ *substantially* from the bodies, or machines, that implement them. According to this view, the concepts that we use to describe mental life, terms like 'pain', 'tickle', 'hope', 'belief', etc. are functional concepts. A concept is functionally individuated, just in case everything falling under that concept does so by virtue of its function. A function is basically a causal role. So, for example, a functionalist in the philosophy of mind would argue that pains are states that are normally caused by tissue damage, and tend in turn to cause avoidance behavior. If we understand that the role of pain is to mediate between tissue damage and various avoidance behaviors, then anything that does this job will count as pain.

Functionalism is not a particularly restrictive view, it simply asserts that most psychological phenomena are what they are by virtue of their place within a causal structure. The structures that the computational functionalists had in mind were modeled on computer programs. A line in a computer program gets its meaning from the role it plays in the program as a whole and, in turn from the role it plays in the behavior of the body or machine that runs that program. Mental states, according to the functionalist, are what they are, by virtue of playing certain causal roles in the world.

For a functionalist, pain is what pain does, or as Dennett often puts it: 'handsome is as handsome does.' Non-philosophers might wonder how we might individuate or identify anything apart from taking its relational properties into account, doesn't Dennett's maxim "handsome is as handsome does" apply to everything? Not according to many philosophers, who believe that a certain subset of objects and phenomena are what they are by virtue of their intrinsic, or non-relational properties. So, while my weight is a relational property, (a property of my relation to other masses in the universe) my mass is not. While this metaphysical distinction between intrinsic and relational (or extrinsic) properties is a topic of considerable controversy, for now, we can assume that something along these lines holds true.

Functionalism, in various guises has dominated the philosophy of mind in the English-speaking world for almost thirty years. This orthodoxy is probably an indication of just how little functionalism really says about the mind. Like most philosophers, Dennett is a functionalist, but where philosophers divide is over the kinds of funcationalism they hold. Dennett's view amounts to a combination of minimal functionalism and methodological behaviorism. This is an intentionally loose characterization of Dennett's position and it introduces two regrettably unwieldy and unstable '–isms'. These two pieces of jargon are introduced here merely as a way of noting where I locate Dennett's work in the tangled metaphysical debates that have characterized traditional philosophy of mind.

Over the years, Dennett has avoided the more extreme versions of both functionalism and behaviorism, for example, he does not believe that the behaviorist's simple Stimulus Response model is sufficient for an explanation of mental phenomena (see e.g., 'Skinner Skinned' in BR). Nor, for example does he believe in the kind of computational functionalism that sees mental life as a matter of manipulating symbols in a language of thought. (see e.g., 'Mid-term examination: Compare and Contrast' in IS). Instead, Dennett has been concerned with the emergence of mind as a problem to be solved scientifically rather than through metaphysics. He has therefore avoided engaging in what he calls the *slogan-honing* of mainstream, metaphysical philosophy of mind. This does not mean that he fails to recognize the depth and interest of the mind-body problem or the important lessons of movements like functionalism. Rather, Dennett sees much of the debate in recent philosophy of mind as far too removed from the genuine empirical questions where progress is likely to be made.

As we shall see in Chapter Two, Dennett is a philosophical naturalist. While it is possible to treat naturalism as a doctrine, in Dennett's case, it is best to understand it as a method. The philosophical naturalist believes that philosophical problems can be solved through a combination of scientific inquiry and the adjustment of our conceptual prejudices in light of empirical evidence. These days most philosophers share a broadly naturalistic perspective. As a result, an introduction to the thought of a naturalist like Dennett runs the risk of simply repeating what most philosophers think they already believe. The challenge is to demonstrate how naturalism can change the way we understand some of the traditional issues in the philosophy of mind. Eliot Sober puts the challenge as follows:

> Advocating naturalism in epistemology often combines the good vibes and gross vacuity that one finds in food commercials on television. A theory of knowledge, like a carton of yogurt, measures up only insofar as it contains no artificial ingredients. I do not doubt that we are organisms, the product of organic evolution and I accept that what knowledge we have is not guaranteed us by a God who is no deceiver...The challenge to naturalism is to show how that point of view changes the contour of problems. (Sober 1985, 165)

Dennett's work meets this challenge convincingly. One of the most striking aspects of Dennett's work is how significantly the *contour of problems* has changed in his work. In some cases this contour seems to have changed so much that Dennett is criticized for straying too far from the traditional characterization of problems in the philosophy of mind. Critics frequently complain that Dennett's accounts of phenomena like consciousness or free will leave out what they believe to be the crucial properties of those notions. According to his critics Dennett should be working on the really hard problems like the nature of phenomenal consciousness or the *what-it's likeness* of conscious experience rather than wasting his time on robots and evolutionary biology. However, appreciating the impact of naturalism is, in large part, a matter of seeing how deeply it changes the way we see problems in the philosophy of mind. As we shall see, for instance, a naturalistic perspective allows one to escape many of the intractable problems that had haunted philosophers of yore.

2

Behaviorism, Naturalism and Ordinary Language Philosophy

This chapter provides some of the scientific and philosophical background to Dennett's contributions to the philosophy of mind. As we shall see, his work is a uniquely fertile combination of three major philosophical movements.

Dennett as Natural Philosopher

Unlike so much of the dry, technical prose one finds in modern philosophy, Daniel Dennett's writing is frank, witty and well-written. Dennett often persuades using stories and jokes rather than formal arguments. In the introduction to his important volume *Dennett and his Critics* Bo Dahlbom writes:

> When other philosophers use definitions and arguments, Daniel Dennett will make his point by telling a story. So if you ask him about his view on a specific question, he will scratch his beard and hem and haw, but only for a few seconds before going into narrative mode, launching into a wonderful story. His philosophy is in his stories. (DAC, 1)

14

While Dennett's use of stories (or 'intuition pumps' as he calls them) may be rhetorically useful, it has run the risk of concealing the underlying unity of his thought. He sometimes gives the impression that with each issue, or problem, we are seeing the fresh application of his very American kind of commonsense. However, as I hope to show, over the past thirty years, his writings and lectures have presented a comprehensive and unified view of the mind.

Dennett's views on particular issues in the philosophy and science of mind have been developing and changing over the years. This, when combined with the complexity of his work on specific issues in the philosophy of mind and his avoidance of *metaphilosophy* (the inquiry into the nature of philosophical theories) makes it difficult for commentators to get a good fix on his philosophical position. Unlike many philosophers of cognitive science, Dennett's philosophy is not entirely a matter of analyzing or criticizing the theories, arguments and concepts of scientists or other philosophers. Instead, he hopes to understand and explain the phenomena that we ordinarily call *mental*. In an interview with neuroscientist Michael Gazzaniga, Dennett says:

> I aspire to create, defend, and confirm (or disconfirm) theories that are directly about the phenomena, not about theories about the phenomena. The philosophers' meta-criticisms are often important clarifiers and exposers of confusion, and as such are – or should be – unignorable contributions, but I myself would also like to make more direct contributions to theory. (Gazzaniga 1997, 176)

Dennett's attention to the phenomena, rather than to theories about the phenomena might seem to put him in the role we ordinarily reserve for scientists. One might, for example, think that investigating the relationship between the brain and psychological process is the business of scientists rather than philosophers. However, before the twentieth century, there actually was no rigid professional distinction between scientists and philosophers. In fact, the English term 'scientist' is a relatively modern (nineteenth century) invention and what we now call natural science was traditionally called 'natural philosophy.' Prior to the twentieth century philosophers understood themselves to be uncovering the workings of the natural world by a wide variety of means. For example, seventeenth and eighteenth century thinkers like Descartes and Leibniz, who are generally read today for their work in metaphysics and epistemology, were among the leading figures of their time in mathematics, biology, physics etc. The

15

distinction between science and philosophy is so new in fact, that some of the more traditional British and Irish universities continue to grant degrees in 'natural philosophy' to students majoring in physics, chemistry and biology. Dennett understands his own work on the model of this older tradition and as a natural philosopher, he is actively involved in the design of experiments, he has collaborated with researchers in the development of a proto-sentient robot *Cog,* his work has spawned a number of important research programs in cognitive science and has contributed significantly to the study of animal minds.

While Dennett is one of the new cadre of philosophers who see their work as fully engaged with the scientific problems of our time, he is also sensitive to the philosophical assumptions and problems underlying the return to philosophy as *natural* philosophy. These problems are most pronounced when it comes to the study of ethics and psychology. As described below, there has been a persistent conceptual divide between modern science and what we ordinarily think of as mental life. So, while Dennett is an active participant in the scientific investigation of mental life, he has also responded to this fundamental philosophical or conceptual problem.

His response to the gap between science and the mind is informed by the lessons of three broad movements: behaviorism, philosophical naturalism and ordinary language philosophy. This chapter discusses these influences and introduces some of the problems that Dennett's philosophy is meant to overcome.

Behaviorism

Dennett is often criticized as being too closely aligned with a movement in philosophy and psychology known as behaviorism. Behaviorism is widely associated with the work of Harvard psychologist B. F. Skinner. Skinner was one of the most important advocates of behaviorism in the United States. He argued that most of what we think of as mental life is simply a complicated set of habits that could be learned or unlearned. These habits could, in principle, be explained in terms of the physiology of the nervous system, hence there is no real need, according to Skinner to bother with psychological or mental processes. In effect, giving up reference to psychological processes means giving up all mention of inner life. Sentences that mentioned thoughts, beliefs, desires, feelings and consciousness were meaningful for the behaviorists only insofar as they could be converted into the terms of stimulus-response psychology.

Skinner's behaviorism is widely thought to be a dehumanizing and unrealistic view of human life and philosophers and scientists have provided powerful arguments against it. In fact, Dennett has also presented a number of important criticisms of Skinner's behaviorism ('Skinner Skinned', 'A Cure for Common Code').

Dennett objects to the central philosophical premise on which behaviorisms like Skinner's were based: "The claim is that *behavioral science proves that people are not free dignified morally responsible agents.*" (BR, 54) In 'Skinner Skinned' Dennett shows that Skinner's grounds for believing this were thoroughly flawed. For Dennett, those parts of our moral and mental lives whose existence Skinner denied are precisely the phenomena that he sees himself in the business of explaining. Dennett believes that we are conscious, morally responsible agents and that we have something like an inner mental life (though, as we shall see, it looks rather different from the traditional model of mental life). For Dennett, these are phenomena to be explained rather than dismissed. However, it remains correct to view Dennett as a behaviorist only insofar as he holds a set of reasonable scientific principles with respect to the investigation of mental life. These principles are certainly due in large part to the behaviorist movement in psychology.

Skinner is the most famous figure in a long line of behaviorist psychologists. Early in the twentieth century many psychologists, especially in the Anglo-American tradition, abandoned the idea of a separate mental stuff that was unavailable to public observation or measurement. Instead, they attempted to explain human and animal behavior entirely in terms of measurable responses to external stimuli. The term 'behaviorism' was introduced by the American psychologist John Watson. (1913) Watson argued that behavior is properly understood as a physiological reaction to environmental stimuli.

Rather than attempting to explore mysterious, inner mental processes, behaviorists sought to establish a firm scientific foundation for psychology. The famous conditioned-reflex experiments of the Russian physiologist Ivan Pavlov along with similar work by American psychologist Edward Thorndike allowed behaviorists to study the relationship between changes in an animal's environment and changes in its behavior in a quantifiable and objective manner. Motivated by what they saw as strict scientific principles, these psychologists sought to explain behavior without recourse to the dubious models of what prior psychologists thought might have been going on inside the minds of their subjects (Watson 1913). And for much of the twentieth century behaviorist psychologists believed that their experimental work demonstrated that it is unnecessary to use terms like belief, desire, representation, mental imagery etc.

However, even at the peak of their influence, behaviorists had difficulty suppressing demands for an explanation of complex mental phenomena like memory and linguistic ability. The experimental exploration of memory offers an excellent illustration of the difficulties faced by classical behaviorism. Early in the twentieth century, behaviorism superseded the older tradition of memory research stemming from the work of German psychologist Hermann Ebbinghaus in the nineteenth century. Unlike the older psychological tradition, behaviorists hoped to avoid the use of unreliable introspective and spoken reports of subjects. And indeed, by the 1920's they had shown the effectiveness of their studies of learning and memory in controlled settings with rats, pigeons and other animals. Their work led them to argue that memory did not function like a file-cabinet or a library that stores representations of past events. They had shown that very simple forms of memory could be explained without recourse to mental representations. In place of mental representations, they posited a single mechanism - the combination of simple reflexes - as the basis of learning. For the behaviorists, memory could be explained as a set of unconscious habits.

While this view of memory was never completely discredited, psychologists soon recognized that matters were considerably more complicated in practice than this simple model seemed to admit. Eventually the behaviorists were forced to admit that they were unable to tame the complexity of the nervous system with their simple model of stimulus and response. Unlike the kind of simple reflex arcs that connect the tap of your doctor's little hammer below your kneecap on the patellar tendon to the involuntary jerk of your leg muscle, the ordinary process of remembering something as simple as a phone number involves an extraordinarily complex tangle of neural connections in the brain with feedback and feedforward activity across large areas of cortex and hippocampus. The complexity of the brain is staggering. And so, while they argued that the reduction of mental life to physiological habits was still correct in principle, the behaviorists soon recognized the necessity of including certain theoretical abstractions in their models that linked stimulus and response.

While some behaviorists (like Skinner) argued that we could ignore the complex internal biology of the organism and treat it simply as a kind of black-box, this view was widely rejected. The weakness of this "empty-organism" view lay in the problem of connecting descriptions of behavior with the mental phenomena that psychologists claimed to be addressing. So for instance, if one ignores the internal biological mechanisms at play in the organism and takes the organism's behavior as one's only source of evidence, one soon faces a problem known as the defeasability of behaviorist reduction.

The behaviorist reductions of mental terms are unreliable because they are so easily defeated by counterexamples. Say, for example, a behaviorist considers a mental state like 'wanting to eat cheese.' The behaviorist cannot refer to desires in his theory, since desire *per se* is not an observable, let alone measurable phenomenon. However, the behaviorist can redefine or *reduce* the mental state to a description of behavioral tendencies. So for example, he could say that the mentalistic description

'the organism wants to eat cheese'

could be translated into the scientifically more respectable description of the organism's behavior:

'if in the presence of cheese, the organism will eat it'.

The trouble with this kind of translation is that it will always be subject to conditions that can lead to its failure. For instance, a subject might really want to eat the cheese, but might be prevented from eating all dairy products for ethical or health reasons. Unfortunately, for the behaviorist, all attempts to convert descriptions of mental states into descriptions of tendencies to behave in certain ways are subject to this kind of problem.

While the behaviorist tradition faces considerable philosophical problems, the historical reasons for the decline of classical behaviorism, can be traced directly to its failure to explain the open-ended flexibility and contextual nature of memory. In his famous maze experiments, Edward Tolman was driven to supplement the behaviorist basics, with hypothetical cognitive maps. Rats, he showed, must have something like a *map* in their brain that they could refer to independently of simple conditioning. Tolman's work challenged the idea that memory could be reduced to habit. He believed that patterns of stimulus and response (SR) play some role in learning as was confirmed by his T-maze experiments. But these experiments also showed SR learning and cognitive mapping to be different forms of learning. A rat can find his way in a maze even when the conditions that governed his training do not fit the circumstances of its behavior in later trials. Those who argued for the necessity of including representations in psychological explanation were encouraged to develop more elaborate internal processing models by Tolman's theory that rats possess mental maps of their environment.

It is unclear exactly what a mental map or representation might be. But while this notion bears a strong resemblance to the mentalistic phenomena that the behaviorists had originally worked to expel, psychologists like Tolman saw these abstractions as the only way of accounting for the patterns they discovered in their study of behavior.

Cognitive psychology emerged as a discrete field of study in the early 1960's in response to what were seen as the failures of behaviorism and yet, many of the important tenets of behaviorism; the commitment to quantifiable evidence and controlled experimental settings continue to guide psychology to this day. While behaviorism is widely regarded as having been discredited by the development of scientific methods for the study of mental or cognitive phenomena, methodological behaviorism still provides an important constraint in scientific practice.

Dennett's approach to the mind owes a great deal to the philosophical principles that underlie what the behaviorists called 'objective psychology'. However, Dennett's behaviorism, like Tolman's acknowledges the impossibility of reducing all useful psychological generalizations to patterns of stimulus and response. Both Tolman and Dennett recognized the necessity of introducing certain theoretical constructs in the explanation of behavior. Theoretical constructs like the mental maps that Tolman invokes in the explanation of his experiments are posited as indispensable ways of tracking the regular patterns of behavior in a complex biological system. In both Dennett and Tolman, these theoretical constructs are not necessarily intended to stand for a map-like neural process in the brain of the rat. Dennett takes great pains to characterize these theoretical constructs in such a way as to avoid having them thought of as hypotheses about mechanisms in the brain. For Dennett, as we shall see, Tolman's mental maps are part of a technique that he labels *heterophenomenology*. In Chapter Five we will investigate this method in detail and examine the status of the kinds of hypothetical entities that Dennett and Tolman posit.

The apparent failure of behaviorism and the rise of cognitive psychology encouraged philosophers like Jerry Fodor to assume that the theoretical constructs of psychology must be thought of as mechanisms in the animal's mind-brain. This is what we shall call a *realistic* interpretation of the theoretical constructs that psychology generates. For example a realistic interpretation of Tolman's mental map might lead one to seek a map-like process or area of cortex in the brain. In Chapter Four we will examine the reasons why the realistic interpretation is not warranted.

Philosophical Naturalism

Dennett is one of the most important representatives of a tradition known as philosophical naturalism. Naturalists basically argue that science and philosophy should not be sharply distinguished, that they are two continuous theoretical enterprises. For Dennett, as for the greatest American philosopher, W. V. Quine, philosophy does not stand apart from our engagement with the natural world. There is no privileged standpoint, or 'first philosophy', that can permit us to discover or determine the rules for natural science, for aesthetics, politics or even ethics apart from an engaged practical acquaintance with these pursuits. Philosophers, according to Dennett, Quine and other naturalist thinkers, simply don't have access to the kinds of *a priori* truths (propositions that are true apart from experience) that can allow us to regulate or legislate the scope and content of human knowledge.

While some philosophers, like Rudolf Carnap, in the first half of the twentieth century held deep admiration for science and attempted to model their work on what they perceived to be the scientific method, philosophy and science were still widely regarded as fundamentally different in kind before the nineteen fifties. Carnap (and many others) believed, that philosophers are primarily in the business of analyzing and explaining the meanings of important concepts. Conceptual analysis of various forms, it was taught, could be practiced without the need for experimental results of any kind. Therefore, at least in principle, philosophy could take place in almost complete ignorance of natural science. This view of philosophy had already begun to collapse by the time Dennett began working in the 'sixties. Some years earlier, Quine had decisively undermined the notion that philosophers working on the meanings of concepts were engaged in a qualitatively different kind of enterprise from scientists working in their laboratories. Quine focussed his criticism on Rudolf Carnap's notion that philosophers uncovered analytic or purely conceptual truths as opposed to the synthetic or empirical truths of the natural sciences. The assumption that certain statements were analytically true (true by virtue of their meanings alone) had seemed to provide a way for philosophers to carve out a useful niche for themselves in the service of science. For example, a statement like 'all bachelors are unmarried males' seemed

21

like the kind of truth that one could discover apart from any scientific research. The concept 'unmarried male' seems included in the concept 'bachelor' in such a way as to render the statement 'all bachelors are unmarried males' true by meaning alone. Philosophy, according to the view of many philosophers before Quine, was the investigation and discovery of such analytically true statements.

In his classic paper 'Two Dogmas of Empiricism,' (1954) Quine showed that there is no special kind of knowledge to which philosophers have some privileged access. Roughly speaking, he argued that no non-circular account of analyticity can be provided that would justify the claim that a statement can be true by virtue of its meaning alone. For, if one claims that analytic truths are sentences that are true on the strength of their meanings, then the question becomes, what is the definition of meaning. Quine argued that an attempt to pin down the notion of meaning leads us back to analyticity and that there is therefore no non-circular definition of analytic truth. According to Quine, this means that the notion of analytic truth crumbles. Through his criticism of the 'analytic-synthetic' distinction, Quine brought the traditional dream of a distinctly philosophical kind of knowledge to an end.

While there are many important and valuable attempts to resuscitate the analytic-synthetic distinction, few philosophers would wish to return to the inflated self-image that some had once endorsed. The post-Quinean world is a far cry from the days when philosophy was understood to provide the rules according to which science should be practiced and when, for example, philosophers like Hegel could confidently predict the impossibility of there being a ninth planet on the strength of his dialectical logic. Hegel's embarrassing prediction was the result of his belief that philosophers had a deeper, or more certain grasp of reality than those who study the natural world empirically. These days, philosophers are wary of making this kind of mistake.

According to naturalists like Dennett and Quine, philosophers and scientists are engaged in the collective human struggle to understand. This continuity has the practical effect of allowing philosophers to apply empirical results to the solution of traditional philosophical problems. More specifically, the naturalist believes that all of reality, including mental life, ethics and culture, can be understood as part of a single natural order. Nothing in nature, according to the naturalist needs to be explained by reference to something that falls outside of the causal order of nature.

Naturalists reject the idea that there is a kind of knowledge, *a priori knowledge*, which cannot be corrected or rejected in light of future evidence. All knowledge comes to us through our dealings with the natural world and there are no divine revelations or philosophical intuitions that can underpin our claims. While this view is widespread among philosophers in our time, Dennett is one of naturalism's most important and consistent representatives.

Naturalism is most radical when it comes to the explanation of mental life. Philosophers who criticize naturalism argue that science will never be able to explain the mind. Instead, they argue, the knowledge of ourselves that we achieve either through the privileged methods of philosophical inquiry or via common sense can serve as an indubitable foundation for all other knowledge. Dennett's naturalism is directly opposed to the idea that philosophers can discover the limits of science a priori. However, unlike many of his naturalist colleagues, Dennett is wary of assuming that we must always privilege science over common sense. For Dennett, scientists are as prone to making conceptual blunders and logical errors as anyone else. So, while philosophers no longer claim dominion over natural science, it is also the case that natural science is subject to revision and cannot be the final arbiter of all things. In his *Darwin's Dangerous Idea* Dennett writes:

> Scientists sometimes deceive themselves into thinking that philosophical ideas are only, at best, decorations or parasitic commentaries on the hard, objective triumphs of science, and that they themselves are immune to the confusions that philosophers devote their lives to dissolving. But there is no such thing as philosophy-free science; there is only science whose philosophical baggage is taken on board without examination. (DDI 21)

So, for Dennett, philosophers should assume that science is fallible and can be corrected. And yet, the ways in which a naturalist philosopher might be able to correct natural scientists are quite different from traditional philosophical criticisms or interventions in scientific practice. For the naturalist, science is not answerable to any superscientific tribunal. Surely then, only science can correct science? What then is the status of philosophy for Dennett? Should philosophers simply pack up their offices and retire?

Naturalists consider philosophy to be continuous with natural science and argue that there is no principled way to distinguish the claims of a philosopher from those of a physicist or a biologist. Philosophers should be equipped with an education in the methods and content of natural science and should bring to this education a level of critical detachment and skepticism that allows him to perform an informed examination of fundamental issues and problems in the natural sciences. At its best, philosophy is the practice of thinking through the consequences of our inherited scientific worldview. It is the informed reflection of science on its own workings. Rather than attempting to determine the principles or logical framework that scientific research must obey, the naturalist philosopher is an active participant in scientific practice. Part of this participation involves the criticism of certain scientific practices or research programs, but this criticism, if it is to be worthwhile, should be informed by scientific practice. Dennett would therefore agree that philosophy and science are, as Quine put it, *reciprocally contained.*

> There is thus reciprocal containment, though containment in different senses: epistemology in natural science and natural science in epistemology...We are after an understanding of science as an institution or process in the world, and we do not intend that understanding to be any better than the science which is its object. This attitude is indeed one that Neurath was already urging in his Vienna Circle days, with his parable of the mariner who has to rebuild his boat while staying afloat in it. (Quine 1969, 84)

A careful study of Dennett's philosophy doubles as an introduction to a naturalist tradition that spans at least the past fifty years in the United States. To understand Dennett's work is to understand what it means to do philosophy on Neurath's boat. He shows how we can do without all claims to eternal and incorrigible principles in our consideration of such important questions as the nature of the human mind, personal identity, value and ethics.

However, Dennett's naturalism is tempered by his association with another major philosophical tradition – ordinary language philosophy. As we shall see, the combination of these two movements marks Dennett as a unique figure in contemporary philosophy.

Ordinary Language Philosophy

In the early pages of his first book *Content and Consciousness* Dennett suggests that the English philosopher Gilbert Ryle had provided a way to escape the problem of mind-body dualism. Ryle was one of the foremost proponents of what has come to be called ordinary language philosophy. The principal figures in the ordinary language tradition; Ludwig Wittgenstein, John Austin and Gilbert Ryle, are united by an interest in the ways words are commonly used. While Wittgenstein is correctly understood as providing the inspiration for much of the work done in this tradition, the term 'ordinary language philosophy' is generally associated with Oxford philosophers of the 1950s and 1960s. Ordinary language philosophy was still an important force during Dennett's time at Oxford in the mid-sixties. The basic idea of this tradition is that philosophical theories and more specifically the philosophical use of terms can be evaluated through a comparison with ordinary usage. While ordinary language philosophy is generally out of favor these days, it has had a significant influence on many of the most important contemporary movements and thinkers in philosophy.

Ryle's *The Concept of Mind* (1949) has become one of the classic works of twentieth century philosophy. It can justifiably be called the founding work in modern philosophy of mind. In it, Ryle attacked what he calls 'Cartesian dualism' or the myth of 'the Ghost in the Machine', arguing that the mind-body problem, the problem of trying to understand the nature of mind and its relationship with the body arises from a 'category mistake'. Chapter Three examines the nature of 'category mistakes' and describes the pivotal role played by the insights of ordinary language philosophers like Ludwig Wittgenstein and Gilbert Ryle in Dennett's philosophy.

Ryle was principally concerned with the ways philosophers misuse language. If we properly understand the ways we ordinarily use terms like *knowledge, mind, will, consciousness* and the like, philosophical puzzles would dissolve. Dennett takes some of the most valuable insights from the ordinary language tradition, but at the end of the day, he sees the mind-body problem as a challenge to science. While it is vital to reflect upon the ordinary ways we use words, this alone will not help us to understand some of the most puzzling aspects of mental life. Dennett's interest in scientific explanation leads him to develop a naturalistic approach to the philosophy of mind that is quite unlike the kind of philosophy we find in Ryle. While Dennett is one of the few prominent exponents of the Rylean approach in the philosophy of mind, the most remarkable aspect of his work to date has been its ability to bring our best science and philosophy into dialogue with one another. Dennett's appreciation for the natural sciences distinguishes him markedly from ordinary language philosophers like Wittgenstein, Ryle and John Austin. Nevertheless, the ordinary language tradition informs much of Dennett's work and has allowed him the conceptual resources to solve some of the most difficult problems in philosophy of mind.

> Both Ryle and Wittgenstein were quite hostile to the idea of a scientific investigation of the mind, and standard wisdom in the "cognitive revolution" is that we have seen through and beyond their ruthlessly unscientific analyses of the mental. Not true. One has to tolerate their often frustrating misperception of good scientific questions, and their almost total ignorance of biology and brain science, but they still managed to make deep and important observations that most of us are only now getting into position to appreciate. (KM, 169)

Distinctions made at the level of ordinary language, for example, Ryle's distinction between "knowing how" and "knowing that" often have considerable value in cognitive science. However, the analysis of ordinary language only goes so far. At a certain point we must be prepared to revise our philosophical prejudices and the customary use of words in light of the evidence of our best science.

3

The Status of Folk Psychology

For Dennett, mental life, like any other natural phenomenon, can become a topic for scientific investigation. And yet, the scientific investigation of mind encounters a number of uniquely philosophical problems. For starters, while few of us could tell a quark from a gluon, or explain the difference between acetylcholine and dopamine, almost all of us believe we possess some acquaintance with minds. At the very least, we believe that we know our own minds with an unusual degree of intimacy and certainty. As it turns out, our confidence rests on rather shaky grounds. As we shall see, it is possible to show that most of what we say and think about minds is, by the very strictest scientific and logical standards, false. And yet, it seems crazy to deny the truth of a large portion of our folk psychological statements. Crazy or not, many scientists and philosophers have denied that our talk of things like belief and desire can make any real scientific sense.

While denying that we have beliefs and desires might seem far-fetched, it is worth considering whether our confidence in the usual ways we speak and write about the mind is appropriate. Do we really know what we are talking about when we talk about the mind? There are reasons to believe that we do not. While we have reasonably well-defined ways of characterizing or identifying the meaning of terms like *electron, shoe* or *egg* folk psychological notions like *belief, desire, thought,* and *mind* are far more difficult to determine.

Intentionality and the Propositional Attitudes

Like most scientists and philosophers, Dennett thinks we have good reason to believe that everything that exists is material. The basic idea behind the materialist assumption is that only those things composed of the entities that existed at the origin of the universe have any relevance to scientific explanation. If we deny this assumption then we will be forced to admit the possibility of supernatural forces and miracles of various kinds coming into play over the course of natural history.

This kind of materialism has served science well. However, mental life presents problems for the science in at least two ways. The first results from a property known as intentionality. Intentionality is the property that certain phenomena (thoughts, words, beliefs, desires) possess, whereby they seem to be about something beyond themselves. For example, Jane's belief that Prague is beautiful is *about* Prague. However this important characteristic of beliefs is difficult to explain in physical terms since 'aboutness' does not seem to be a physical relation in the ordinary sense. A rock or a puddle cannot be said to be *about* anything, whereas, a belief or a desire is, perhaps by definition, always directed towards something other than itself.

Consider desire. Most of our desires are desires for something or another. Picture yourself wanting an item of food, a beautiful mate or a new computer. Perhaps you imagine your desires like an invisible hand stretching forth from your mind into the world to grasp the desired object. When we experience desire, we tend to feel it as a need for something beyond ourselves. The term 'intentionality', is meant to capture this quality of mental life. It derives from the medieval Latin *intentio*. *Intentio* literally means a tension or stretching forth and it was taken by some medieval philosophers to be one of the characteristic properties of mental entities. Of course, *intentionality* in this context should be distinguished from our ordinary use of the word *intentional*. By using the term *intentionality* in this technical context, philosophers don't mean to imply that the distinguishing feature of mental phenomena is that they are done on purpose. Instead, intentionality is understood to be the distinctive ability of beliefs, desires and other mental notions to be *about* something.

28

In his *Psychology from an Empirical Standpoint* (1874) Austrian psychologist and philosopher Franz Brentano reintroduced the notion of intentionality into modern philosophy with the claim that:

> Every mental phenomenon is characterized by what the scholastics of the Middle Ages referred to as the intentional (and also mental) inexistence of the object, and what we, although with not quite unambiguous expressions, would call relation to a content, direction upon an object (which is not here to be understood as a reality) or immanent objectivity. (Brentano [1874] 1973: 88)

Brentano offered intentionality or *aboutness* as the defining characteristic or mark of mental life. All and only mental entities are intentional entities, according to Brentano. Objects in the physical world and the objects that we desire, or about which we have beliefs, are not *about* anything he argued (with the sole exception of those occasions where we theorize about the intentional status of our own thoughts). A belief, a hope or a desire must be about something, whereas non-intentional objects like rocks, trees, continents, etc. are not about anything. Non-intentional objects just are. While Brentano's view is quite subtle and does not simply divide the world into physical and mental phenomena in the stark way my thumbnail sketch implies, he was understood in the Anglo-American tradition to have provided a simple criterion for doing precisely this.

Prior to Dennett's work in his 'Intentional Systems' (1971) the debate on intentionality was marked by two basic alternatives. These two positions, represented by Chisholm on the one hand and Quine on the other, take their starting point from the same basic insight. Both Quine and Chisholm claim that our talk about mental life cannot be integrated into the scientific worldview. For Quine this meant that we should eliminate talk of the mental from philosophical and scientific discourse. According to Quine, such talk was an 'essentially dramatic idiom' devoid of scientific value. (WO 219) For Chisholm, by contrast, it meant that there was no way that science could ever explain mental life in terms of more basic scientific phenomena. The trouble with Chisholm's position, at least for philosophical naturalists like Quine and Dennett, is that is seems to divide the world in two. On the one hand, we have the world as described by science, on the other hand we have the realm of mental entities that elude scientific explanation. This kind of dualism is anathema to naturalists. However, while Quine famously dismissed the possibility that we might integrate talk of belief

29

and desire into our scientific worldview, his dismissal came with the acknowledgement of the 'practical indispensibility' of the intentional idiom.

The 'intentional idiom' was Quine's term for our ordinary talk about subjects like belief, desire, hope, thought, and the like. When we explain the actions of people, animals and some machines (including the explanations we provide to ourselves about our own actions) we almost inevitably employ this intentional idiom. If, for example, I'm explaining why Fred brought his umbrella to work, I will refer to psychological states, such as his belief that it is likely to rain and his desire to stay dry. An attempt to explain human action without calling on the intentional idiom soon confirms its practical indispensability. Quine and Dennett both recognize the "practical indispensability of the intentional idiom". They both realized that it was an invaluable part of our daily lives. Practically speaking, it would be virtually impossible to do without some reference to belief, desire and other intentional notions. However, Quine was quite explicit in his denial of the meaningfulness of talk about intentionality. For Quine, Chisholm's demonstration of the irreducibility of intentionality demonstrated the "baselessness of intentional idioms and the emptiness of a science of intention." (Quine 1960, 221) It is useful to outline the basic tension between science and intentionality at this stage.

Philosophers sometimes characterize the intentional idiom as a kind of folk theory. The idea being that our explanations and predictions of human behavior are like our explanations and predictions of the objects in the natural world. Just as there are theories that explain the motion of the planets, we have another, perhaps less sophisticated, theory that explains human behavior. This theory, according to certain philosophers, consists of beliefs, desires and other so-called *propositional attitudes*. These propositional attitudes have a set of predictable causal relations that permit us to explain human action. In the case mentioned above, Fred's belief that it is likely to rain, when combined with his desire to stay dry *caused* the action of taking his umbrella to work.

For all their usefulness, beliefs, desires and other propositional attitudes have a peculiar place in our picture of the world. On the one hand, they seem indispensable. However, at the same time, beliefs, desires and thoughts, like ghosts, mermaids and angels fail to meet some of our basic criteria for scientifically respectable existence. What, after all, is a belief? We can't cut a belief in two, nor can we weigh or touch one. And yet, there seems to be no denying that people have beliefs. So, if science is our way of determining what genuinely exists

30

and if the propositional attitudes seem to fall outside of the purview of science, we seem to be faced with a problem. This is the problem that Dennett has devoted much of his life to solving.

Quine has given the clearest presentation of the real heart of the problem in its modern form. While he recognized their importance in everyday life, Quine showed that the propositional attitudes were useless for science. Here's why. First, say I have a scientific theory.

Let's say that my theory contains the following statement:

> (A) "If Freddy Mercury comes to town there will be a commotion"

Notice that this peculiar little sentence contains no propositional attitudes, no mention of belief, desire, thought and the like. Given this statement as part of my wider theory I can make a number of perfectly reasonable predictions and inferences. Despite its strangeness, this little law of nature in my imaginary theory has the same logical structure as:

> (B) "If water is brought to 100° Centigrade it will boil"

or

> (C) "If enough snow falls on that branch it will break"

However, as soon as I introduce propositional attitudes into the statements of my theory, trouble ensues. The reason is simple. Given for instance:

> (D) "Jean believes that Freddy Mercury was the lead singer for Queen"

We cannot infer with certainty that

> (E) "Jean believes that Farookh Bulsara was the lead singer for Queen"

This is the case despite the little known fact that Freddy Mercury and Farookh Bulsara were the same person. As all die-hard fans know, Bulsara changed his name to Freddy Mercury in order to make himself more acceptable to a British audience. Jean, of course, may not be a fan and may never have heard the name Farookh Bulsara, therefore (E) may not be true. So, (D) and (E) are not interchangeable, by virtue of containing propositional attitudes.   But now consider our original statement (A) above, the one that contained no mention of propositional attitudes:

> (A) "If Freddy Mercury comes to town there will be a commotion"

If this is true, then it will also be true that

> (A*) "If Farookh Bulsara comes to town there will be a commotion"

In (A) and (A*) we are referring to a particular physical object – a man – whose presence is likely to cause a commotion, whereas in (D) and (E) we are referring to a something far more problematic, the propositional attitude *belief that*.   Quine argued that this failure of substitutivity in (D) and (E) is enough to vitiate all theories that include propositional attitudes and that, if we want good science, the very least we can ask for is that the law of substitutivity hold.   Therefore, according to Quine we should eliminate talk of propositional attitudes from our science.

Eliminativism

Quine's proposal that we eliminate talk of the mind from our scientific discourse had few takers.   The emergence of cognitive psychology in the 1960's seemed to lend a degree of scientific legitimacy to the study of propositional attitudes. Over the years, philosophers like Jerry Fodor and Fred Dretske argued that we should ignore Quine's criticisms and should treat things like beliefs, desires and other mental entities as objects that we can study using the tools of cognitive psychology, computer science and information theory.   Such thinkers maintain that we have strong reasons to believe that entities like beliefs and desires really exist, and that through cognitive science we can investigate their properties.

However, vocal Quineans like Richard Rorty, Paul Feyerabend, Stephen Stich and the husband and wife team, Paul and Patricia Churchland have continued to urge us to jettison the intentional idiom. The Churchlands have been the most prominent voices in support of the belief that neuroscience will soon replace the ordinary ways we think and talk about the mind.   In his 1981 paper 'Eliminative materialism and propositional attitudes' Paul Churchland argues that we really have

32

no reason to believe that folk psychology is true. He contends that folk psychology is a theory that has had little real success, and that like alchemy and phlogiston theory it has failed to generate scientific progress. According to Churchland, the intentional idiom and more specifically the ordinary folk psychological explanations we provide to account for one another's behavior are, by any standards of scientific truth, simply false. Therefore, like Homer's gods, the entities that folk psychology mentions (beliefs, desires and all the rest) simply don't exist.

The Churchlands believe that a mature science that explains how the brain produces the behavior that interests us will not mention propositional attitudes. This is because a mature scientific psychology will be a genuine science and will therefore obey the principle of substitutivity. Introducing propositional attitudes, as Quine showed, impedes the development of genuine science.

The ultimate presupposition underlying the argument between realists like Fodor and eliminativists like Churchland is the belief that folk psychology constitutes a theory in the same way that, e.g., physics or biology generates theories. Dennett recognized this point early in his career. Both Ryle and Dennett provide ways to circumvent the debate between the eliminativists and the realists by distinguishing various levels of scientific inquiry and theory construction. As we shall see, ordinary language philosophers recognized that the urge to force our ordinary psychological discourse into the mold of strict scientific theorizing is mistaken.

Dennett's middle way

Dennett's middle way is to insist on the truthfulness of much of folk psychology while denying that its truth gives us sufficient reason to believe in the entities that folk psychology putatively mentions. So, just because the statement that Jack believes Tuesday follows Monday is true, it doesn't follow that there exists an entity somewhere in Jack's mind or brain that we can call Jack's belief that Tuesday follows Monday. So, for Dennett, truths of folk psychology do not license us to go looking for entities that correspond to those truths. Dennett denies the principal assumption underlying the debate between Fodor and the Churchlands. For Dennett, folk psychology is not a theory in the same way that, for example, physics or biology generates theories.

Dennett disagrees with Churchland on both the usefulness and the objectivity of folk psychology. We find talk of beliefs, desires and other mental notions practically indispensable in our daily lives. They allow us to get along in the social world, and they help us to organize massively complex biological and artificial systems into manageable and predictable patterns of behavior. Since our way of thinking and talking about minds serves as a powerful tool in a diverse set of contexts, surely, Dennett will argue, we are entitled to believe that most of our ordinary claims about mental notions are as true as any statement of fact can be? Dennett is very sensitive to the peculiar place of folk psychology in relation to the natural sciences. For Dennett, it certainly is not the case that:

(1) Jill believes that protons have a positive charge

is true in the same way that

(2) Protons have a positive charge

is true.

However, what does it mean to say that these two sentences are true in different ways? To understand Dennett's middle way requires attention to the work of ordinary language philosophers like Gilbert Ryle. For philosophers like Ryle and Dennett it is a mistake to hold sentences like (1) and (2) to the same standards of truth. Notions like 'belief' and 'proton' have the same role in the surface grammar of our language- they're both nouns. However this superficial similarity should not lead us to think that sentences involving the term 'belief' refer to beliefs in the same way that sentences containing the term 'proton' refer to protons. To do so, would be an example of what Ryle called a category mistake. The notion of a category mistake was originally introduced as a way of understanding how certain kinds of philosophical problems get started. So, for example, Ryle's analysis of the mind-body problem relied on showing that philosophical problems are generated by illicitly imposing standards of truth from one category or domain on another. As we shall see, the realists and the eliminativists are mistakenly treating ordinary folk psychological statements as though they were inadequate or primitive scientific theories.

Ryle initially explains what he means by a category mistake with an example. Imagine that a foreign visitor to a university is taken on a tour of the campus. After being shown each building in turn, the visitor thanks his host and asks whether he could now be taken to the University. The visitor's request indicates his mistaken assumption that the university, like the library, the classroom buildings and the administration buildings, would also be a building rather than being an institution constituted of the buildings, staff and students that the visitor saw on his tour. The visitor had committed the category mistake of placing 'university', an institution, in the same category as the buildings that jointly house that institution. Category mistakes arise from misunderstandings of the ordinary operation of our language, like trying to send an email to the average taxpayer, or wondering whether there is a particular player responsible for *esprit de corps*. Category mistakes lead to questions that seem nonsensical or funny to competent native speakers of a language. Ryle's examples of what he means by 'category mistake' are all confusions that seem to rest on an inability to use certain items in English vocabulary. And yet, according to Ryle, the philosophically interesting category mistakes that lie at the root of the debates in the philosophy of mind are made by people who are perfectly competent speakers.

According to Ryle, attention to the categories (or "logical types") that emerge from an investigation of ordinary language will show us why the question of the scientific or material status of the mind is not really a problem. When we worry about the relationship between the mind and the body, or the between statements about psychology and statements of the natural sciences, our mistake, according to Ryle, lies in treating statements about mental phenomena in the same way we treat statements about ordinary physical objects. Basically, he argues we have incorrectly treated minds as though they are things. Mental terms, such as 'mind', 'thought' or 'belief', according to Ryle, are not words which refer to, or describe, an inner private mental world of spiritual entities. This view of the mind has a powerful hold on many of us, but, according to Ryle, it is simply the result of a rather basic mistake in early modern philosophy.

He argued that the source of this error lay in Descartes' inability to reconcile his religious and moral convictions with Galileo's hypothesis that every occupant of space could be given a mechanical explanation.

> He and subsequent philosophers naturally but erroneously availed themselves of the following escape-route. Since mental-conduct words are not to be construed as signifying the occurrence of mechanical processes, they must be construed as signifying the occurrence of non-mechanical processes; since mechanical laws explain the movements in space as the effects of other movements in space, other laws must explain some of the non-spatial workings of minds as the effects of other non-

spatial workings of minds... The differences between the physical and the mental were thus represented as differences inside the common framework of the categories of 'thing' (COM, 19)

According to Ryle, the idea that the mind is a kind of para-mechanical system that causes both mental and physical events, is a mistake on a par with the foreigner's confusion with respect to the difference between buildings and institutions in the example above. Descartes had no reason to go looking for a parallel system of mental causes over and above the physical causes that Galileo's mechanistic science would provide. Now this, of course does not mean that Ryle would side with eliminativists like Churchland. Instead, Ryle argued our psychological discourse should be thought of as consisting of dispositional terms derived from the ordinary observation of human behavior. Dispositions are propensities or tendencies to perform a particular action under certain conditions. So, for example, water has a disposition to freeze at temperatures below 32 degrees Farenheidt. Similarly, according to Ryle, to be intelligent is to be disposed to perform well in certain socially specified cognitive tasks. When we say that a child is intelligent, according to Ryle, we are not referring to any particular object or process in her brain, or mind. For Ryle, intelligence is simply the disposition to perform certain tasks successfully.

The right approach to a phenomenon like intelligence is not to look for causes of intelligent behavior. Instead one should ask "By what criteria intelligent behavior is actually distinguished from non-intelligent behavior" (COM, 22) Of course, the focus on criteria is not meant as a denial that mental phenomena are caused by brain events. Obviously, Ryle believed that our brains and behavior are connected. However, brain events (or for that matter Cartesian para-mechanical causes) of our behavior are irrelevant, according to Ryle. When we talk about intelligence, hope or fear, we are talking about certain kinds of behavior and not about phenomena in the tissue of the nervous system. The best way to understand what those 'kinds of behavior' are is to study the criteria we use to distinguish them from one another.

Dennett's middle way between eliminativism and realism arises from this basic Rylean diagnosis of the sources of error in the philosophy of mind. Building on Ryle in the early pages of *Content and Consciousness* Dennett argues that words do not all refer in the same way. "By and large," he writes "words for everyday middle-sized objects fit in the greatest variety of contexts while 'abstract' and 'theoretical' words are the most restricted." (CC, 7) Compare, for

36

example, a word like 'shoe' or 'rock' with a word like 'mile', 'sake' or 'opportunity'. We can buy, sell, stand on, or even eat shoes and rocks, but there is something wrong with the idea of buying sakes or standing on opportunities. Clearly then, there are certain nouns that behave very differently from those that refer to ordinary middle-sized objects.

For Ryle, problems in the philosophy of mind are symptoms of a peculiarly philosophical misuse of language. Philosophers, according to Ryle, are confused about the proper use of terms like 'mind', 'thought' and 'belief' and have mistakenly construed these terms as referring to objects of the same *category* as nouns like 'table', 'house', 'rock' and other medium-sized dry goods. For the young Dennett, if we examine the ordinary use of words like 'opportunity,' 'dint,' 'sake' and the like, we find that words function in a wide variety of ways. Considering the way these words work offers possibilities for thinking about how psychological terms might function in our ordinary folk psychological discourse. However, we might question the analogy between abstract nouns like 'opportunities' and 'centimeters' with psychological terms. After all, thoughts and minds seem to have a much more concrete existence than sakes, miles or dints. (CC, 8) Dennett acknowledges our sense of the reality of these psychological notions. However, his comparison of psychological phenomena with other 'real' things – miles, opportunities, dints etc. – is meant to draw us away from the idea that for a thing to be real, it has to be real in the same way a table or a goose might be real.

In his early work, Dennett takes the ontological status of the mind to be on a par with the ontological status of words like 'voice'. Are there voices? One is inclined to answer 'Of course! We hear and enjoy and recall and recognize voices, so there are voices.' We are convinced that things like voices and minds exist *in some sense*. But what does this *in some sense* amount to? The ordinary language philosophers had hoped to show that different *categories* contain terms that function in different ways. It is simply a mistake, according to the ordinary language philosophers, to treat minds as objects. And once we begin to recognize the difference between different categories of words, we can prevent certain kinds of philosophical questions from arising in the first place.

From the Rylean perspective, the debate between the eliminativists and the realists rests on a basic mistake. However, the curious and problematic thing about ordinary language philosophers is their inability to present the reasons why a particular philosophical debate, and the questions that go along with it are misbegotten. They can attempt to *show* you why the realist/antirealist debate is misbegotten,

37

but they can't *tell* you why it's so. As it turns out, the ordinary language philosopher makes his point by analogy rather than argument. So, for example, in order to demonstrate the confusion underlying the realist/antirealist quest for some object that can legitimately be labeled 'mind', Dennett asks us to imagine a series of questions that a philosophically confused physiologist might ask during his investigation of the voice:

Is the voice identical with the larynx?
No,
Then is it the lungs?
No,
Is it a stream of air?
No.
Is it a sound? No, Then it must be some *other* thing I have not yet examined. (CC,12)

The strategy that ordinary language philosophers employ in their diagnosis of philosophical mistakes is to rule out the questions that give rise to those mistakes by declaring them ill-formed and hence admitting no answer. The physiologist who identifies the voice with the larynx, the lungs or any other ordinary physical object is making a category mistake, according to the Rylean. For Dennett the identification of mind and brain or voice and larynx is fundamentally misguided. By carefully listening to the way we use these terms in our ordinary lives, one recognizes that if voices can be said to exist, they exist in very different ways from lungs and streams of air. In analogous cases in the philosophy of mind, eliminativists like Churchland have tended to opt for the radical solution of simply dispensing with troublesome notions like beliefs and desires. If we take this approach to Dennett's voice/larynx problem, it would mean denying the reality of voices and focusing our study instead on the mechanical and biological process that interested the physiologist in our example. The denial of voices had the advantage "of providing a reason for ruling out the physiologist's questions which are intuitively wrongheaded." (CC, 12) However, for the ordinary language philosophers this would have been an unacceptably high price to pay. Instead of denying the reality of voices, minds, dints, opportunities and the like, they hoped to undertake a detailed investigation of words and families of words. In this way, the categories that structure our language could be revealed and

38

philosophers would have a way of ruling certain kinds of questions and inquiries out of court.

> A voice is not an organ, disposition, process, event, capacity or – as one dictionary definition has is – a 'sound uttered by the mouth'. The word 'voice' as it is discovered in its own peculiar environment of contexts, does not fit neatly the physical, non-physical dichotomy [...] but it is not for that reason a vague or ambiguous or unsatisfactory word. (CC 9)

From Dennett's perspective, 'voice' is a term that cannot be identified in any unproblematic way with the kinds of things that the natural sciences study. We use the word 'voice' in a unique set of contexts and outside of these contexts the term is meaningless. 'Voices' are certainly not the kind of thing that realists and antirealists can legitimately argue about. If Dennett's analogy works, then the same will hold for the mind. The analogy with terms like 'sake', 'dint' 'voice' and the like is meant to shed light on the peculiarity of seeking a straightforward identification of mental phenomena with particular brain states, or with spiritual essences of one kind or another. It is easy to see how asking whether there really are sakes seems to indicate a kind of confusion or misunderstanding. The early Dennett, and the ordinary language tradition before him, had hoped that the analogy between psychological terms and words like 'dint', 'mile' and 'sake' would move readers to recognize the confusion involved in asking whether there really are minds.

The major problem with the ordinary language tradition is exemplified, in the case we are considering, by its dependence upon the reader's ability to recognize the deviant usage of the term 'voice' that is involved in our imaginary physiologist's line of inquiry.

Ordinary language philosophers argued that the very process of elucidating the ordinary use of language would dissolve many long-standing philosophical worries. However, Dennett recognizes that attempts to demonstrate the emptiness of certain lines of inquiry based solely on the recognition that we use language in one way or another are profoundly limited. As he pointed out in *Content and Consciousness*, unless one is immediately convinced by the use of examples in the work of Ryle and others, it will be difficult to find any straightforward logical or conceptual distinction between mental entity terms and physical entity terms that could be used to justify the claim that Descartes' dualism is a 'category mistake.'

Dennett accepted Ryle's account of mental states as being individuated by reference to conventions without accepting that this insight constituted a solution to the problem of mind. Unlike Ryle, who believed that Cartesian dualism was simply the result of a grand philosophical mistake, that could solved once we "rectify the logical geography of the knowledge we already possess" (COM, 7) Dennett recognized the limits of a philosophical method that simply shuffled or rearranged our concepts. For Dennett, the mind-body problem was both a conceptual and a scientific problem.

In the early pages of Dennett's first book, *Content and Consciousness*, dualism is treated as a threat to the core principle of modern science - the principle of conservation of energy.

> If, *ex hypothesi*, mental events are non-physical, they can involve no physical energy or mass, and hence cannot in any way bring about changes in the physical world, unless we are to abandon the utterly central principle of conservation of energy and all its ramifications. (CC, 3)

The principle of conservation of energy states that in a system that does not undergo any force from outside the system, the amount of energy is constant, irrespective of its changes in form. There are important reasons why naturalist philosophers like Dennett emphasize the principle of conservation of energy in their descriptions of the mind-body problem. Modern philosophers eschew supernatural forces of any kind and are therefore eager to understand the place of familiar things like beliefs, hopes and desires in the natural world. The principle of conservation of energy is understood to hold for nature as a whole. Therefore, by arguing that minds are not objects while simultaneously believing that they have some kind of causal relation with the body, one is committed to the denial of the principle of conservation of energy. Accepting the idea that non-physical causes play a significant role in the natural world, is incompatible with the scientific worldview.

While Ryle saw dualism as a category mistake to be dispelled through the analysis of our language, Dennett understood it to be a scientifically objectionable hypothesis that can only be true, if the basic principle of modern science turns out to be false. A simple rearrangement of our conceptual furniture was not sufficient to solve the basic problem that mental life poses for science.

Of course work done in the ordinary language tradition was not merely a discussion of category mistakes. Wittgenstein's reflections on mind and language in *Philosophical Investigations* and elsewhere certainly go beyond mere criticism of the philosophical use of words, providing fertile insights into the texture of psychological notions. Similarly, Ryle's *Concept of Mind* (1949) was not just a criticism of the Mind-Body problem, but also a constructive analysis of some of the basic notions that philosophers of mind now struggle with. However, for the most part, when it came to empirical matters in psychology, philosophers like Ryle tended to defer to behaviorism. As we saw in Chapter Two, by placing their faith in behaviorism, proponents of the ordinary language tradition had bet on the wrong horse.

4

Patterns and Stances

As we have seen, careful consideration of psychological terms soon reveals their peculiar status. While we are almost certain that things like beliefs and desires are real, we are unsure how they exist, or what it means to say that sentences about beliefs are true or false. The problematic status of psychological phenomena, along with the logical difficulties described in the previous chapter, led many psychologists and philosophers to recommend that we ignore folk psychology in favor of the empirically respectable results of the natural sciences. It is difficult to imagine doing without the terms of commonsense psychology, but this is precisely what some important philosophers and scientists have recommended.

In order to avoid what they see as pernicious mentalism, prominent naturalists like Quine and Churchland have argued that we should ignore most of our commonsense beliefs about minds and focus instead on the evidence provided by neuroscience and the study of behavior. The tension that results from needing to talk about the mind and not knowing what it means to talk about the mind forms the core problem that Dennett's philosophy is designed to overcome.

Puzzling questions confront us when we try to remain faithful to both commonsense and the strictest standards of scientific truth: How can we be wrong about the idea that people's actions are caused by their beliefs? Surely it makes little sense to *believe* that there are no beliefs? Furthermore, it is difficult to understand what it would mean to judge whether eliminativism is true, since without intentional notions like belief, it seems unlikely that we could continue to speak meaningfully of truth and falsity. Dennett's philosophical work is devoted, in large part to showing why our ordinary conceptions of mind are both completely reasonable and adequate for most ordinary purposes, and yet, in some more basic sense, incorrect. He explains how we are all simultaneously virtuosos and idiots when it comes to matters of the mind.

To explain how this can be the case, Dennett turns to Darwin. According to Dennett, the words we use to describe mental life are part of a strategy that has evolved for predicting the behaviors of animals and people that are relevant to us. Animals, especially those that live in social groups, must constantly monitor and anticipate the behavior of their fellows. It is important for each to have a reliable way of determining the behavior of its partners in social activity, its prey, potential predators, etc. In our own lives we manage to predict and explain the behavior of other people and animals with relatively high levels of success. We see similar levels of success in the behavior of other species.

It's sometimes tempting to assume that when we manage to make a correct interpretation of the beliefs and desires of an organism it's as though we are able to look inside its mind so as to uncover the truth about the processes and mechanisms at work inside the mind/brain. While this intuition is central to the work of philosophers like Jerry Fodor, (1975) Dennett sees matters differently. For Dennett, when we take the intentional stance towards something or someone, we project the virtual world of beliefs and desires onto the other person or animal in somewhat the same way a geographer might project lines of latitude and longitude onto the Earth's surface. In both cases, the projections permit us a means of manipulating the objects in questions and in both cases the question of whether these virtual objects *really exist* is misguided. Dennett's approach accounts for the ability of animals to make reliable predictions about the behavior of others given their complete ignorance of the biological mechanisms that govern behavior. Since we ordinarily have no access to the internal mechanisms governing the behavior of our fellow creatures, we must adopt what Dennett calls *the intentional stance* towards them. The intentional stance is a strategy that begins with the assumption that other animals believe what they should believe given their perceptions and desire what they should desire given their needs. This is what Dennett calls the assumption of optimal design. We assume that other animals (including people) tend to pursue outcomes that serve their interests and that they have been equipped, by natural selection with suitable perceptual and cognitive capacities to manipulate their environments appropriately. Ascriptions of beliefs and desire are often objectively true, he grants, but not by virtue of describing inner mechanisms, any more than references to centers of gravity, vectors, equators and other useful virtual notions.

The reasons underlying the success of the intentional stance are relatively straightforward. As we saw in the first chapter, Dennett argues that the vicissitudes of life would soon eliminate species that fail to behave in such a way as to perpetuate their species.

The Design Stance

Dennett's 1971 paper 'Intentional Systems' introduced a way of reconciling our talk of beliefs and desires with the scientific worldview. 'Intentional system' is Dennett's term for the kinds of things that folk psychological generalizations help us to predict and control. The notion of an intentional system relies on the distinction between three kinds of interpretive strategies or stances that we can adopt towards the objects in our environment. He often uses the example of a chess computer to illustrate these three stances.

Though its behavioral repertoire is relatively limited, predicting the behavior of a reasonably sophisticated chess computer can still pose quite a challenge. We could begin by adopting what Dennett calls a *design stance* towards the computer. If one understands precisely how the computer was designed, if, for instance one had access to the computer's wiring diagram and to the program that was designed to run on it, then, one could (with extreme difficulty) eventually determine the moves in the game that the computer would make. We usually reserve the design stance for mechanical devices, however, there is also a long tradition of treating biological phenomena along these lines. So, for instance, when we say that the purpose, or function of the heart is to pump blood we are describing a particular subset of biological phenomena in terms of the design stance. In the case of the heart, or some other biological phenomena, we can adopt the design stance without presupposing the existence of a designer. Over time, natural selection shapes biological systems to perform recognizable functions. The reliability of biological functions means that extremely complex biological phenomena are often amenable to the design stance in the absence of any designer.

Of course, the design stance depends on the object in question performing precisely as it was designed. Spilling a little coffee on the chess computer would certainly reduce the likelihood of a successful prediction from the design stance. At this point we must abandon the relative convenience of the design stance and look instead at the details of the physical structure of the phenomenon.

The Physical Stance and the Reductionist Dream

The second of Dennett's interpretive stances is the *physical stance*. This is a description of what Dennett called in his 1971 "the actual physical state of the particular object [...] worked out by applying whatever knowledge we have of the laws of nature. It is from this stance alone that we can predict the malfunction of a system." (BR, 4) According to this view, the physical stance would permit us to understand (at least in principle) what would happen to the computer once the spilled coffee had short-circuited the its wiring.

The idea underlying the account of the physical stance articulated in 'Intentional Systems' rests on a rather old-fashioned picture of physics. The 19th century French physicist Pierre Simon de Laplace, famously suggested the possibility that if one were to know the direction and velocity of every particle of matter at any point in time, it would be possible, given a suitably powerful calculating machine, to determine the state of the universe at any other point in time; we could tell the future and reconstruct the past in every detail. If Laplace's hypothesis could be proven correct, the motion of the physical world, including every motion of our bodies, would be completely predictable and determined by prior states of the universe. By treating nature as an extremely complicated mechanical system governed by the laws of physics, Laplace's hypothesis epitomizes the dream that underlies much of modern science. While 20th century physics has shown that his dream is impossible, Laplace's hypothesis has continued to provide philosophers with a fertile thought experiment and a deep challenge.

The fact that the physics of our own time doesn't support Dennett's 1971 articulation of the physical stance is not of great importance. The physical stance need not be committed to physics turning out one way or another. Instead it can be understood as the idea that scientific problems can almost always be tackled by paying attention to the parts of the system under scrutiny. The weird world of quantum physics aside, most scientific problems can be solved through attention to the interaction between components. So, for example, when Dennett asserts that "[W]e are each *made of* mindless robots and nothing else, no non-physical, non-robotic ingredients at all," (RPI, 3) he is articulating the consequences of an idea that most educated people understand and accept: We are each made of about fifty million million cells and each of these cells can be understood to function like a tiny

45

biological machine. Few of us bother to consider the profound implications of this idea. However, if science tells us that the combined activity of this community of fifty million million tiny machines is sufficient to explain the behavior of a human being, then we should accept that all reference to non-mechanical components or forces is otiose.

The idea that everything about us can, in principle be explained once we understand the operation of our smallest parts is known as reductionism. Reductionism is an old doctrine with a number of important variants in modern philosophy. These range from Ernst Nagel's (1961) idea that every event and property in the universe could, in principle be explained through a logical deduction from the laws and initial conditions of our basic physics, to somewhat more modest *New Wave* versions of reduction as articulated by philosophers like Hooker, Churchland and Bickle. These philosophers claim that all phenomena at the higher level can be shown to be equivalent to certain sets of phenomena at the physical level. The new wave view is equivalent to the idea that no event or property can do anything for which its physical constituents are not responsible.

This second kind of reductionism is compatible with Dennett's philosophical position. However, as we saw earlier, thinkers like Churchland deny the truth of statements that refer to higher-level phenomena and entities. In particular, for Churchland and Bickle, the fact that higher-level phenomena like minds seem to add nothing to the world that wasn't already in place at the more basic physical levels, indicates that these higher-level phenomena are redundant and often misleading freeloaders on our scientific discourse that should be eliminated.

Unlike some other reductionist thinkers, Dennett is concerned to understand how phenomena like belief, desire and value emerge in the natural world. The metaphysical challenge facing a philosopher like Dennett is to understand why there is any point in talking about these notions in a world governed by the laws of physics. In Dennett's case, he has occasionally assumed that, if we knew the actions and interactions of all the cells in a human body, we could, in principle, predict the activity of the body as a whole. However, is it really true that the activity of all these tiny machines suffices to explain all of the richness of human experience and behavior? Unless one wishes to introduce mysterious non-physical forces into one's science, it must be true. We must believe that anything the mind does is the result of some change in the body. But surely, even if we agree with all of this, it's still the case that there's more to life than physics? In practice, the

46

physicist's domain extends no further than the anionic hydrogen atom. Once things get any more complex than this, physics is of little help.

Chemistry and biology, let alone psychology seem to reveal phenomena that are completely unpredictable from the perspective of physics alone. The metaphysical status of things that emerge over the course of natural history has presented a puzzle to philosophers. For example, there was a time in natural history prior to the appearance of biological life, thought and even chemistry. At a certain point in natural history these phenomena came into being. Obviously these new things are composed entirely of the material that preceded them. However, what are we to say of the new level of organization that these interesting emergent phenomena embody? Emergent phenomena are new and interesting by virtue of exhibiting levels of organization or patterns whose appearance was unpredictable from the perspective of physics. Let's return, for the sake of argument, to La Place's impossible fantasy. The position of each particle at every point in time is known to the omniscient. However, according to Dennett, this knowledge would not necessarily allow him to recognize the patterns and structures that these particles comprise. As we shall see below, when we examine Robert Nozick's criticisms of Dennett, an eliminativist perspective misses valuable and informative patterns whose novel properties are not predictable given the laws of physics alone.

According to the eliminativist these new patterns are basically irrelevant. Since they are composed solely of material phenomena and since matter is governed by the laws of physics, all we really need in order to predict and control the universe are physical laws and initial conditions. Eliminativist philosophers rely on the idea that putatively emergent properties or entities are causally preempted by the underlying physics. So, while we can certainly identify new patterns and phenomena for instrumental or other reasons they can only be shown to be 'real' or, using the jargon; to constitute a 'natural kind', given the identification of a unique set of causal powers. Given the assumption that the physical world is causally closed (causal closure is the idea that the only things in the physical world that can cause things to happen are physical things) it is difficult to think of causal powers that are not exhaustively captured by the power of the physical constituents.

Dennett's response to this dilemma has wavered somewhat over the years. While his position has softened recently, he is famous for his early denials that mental terms refer to objects that possess causal power. (1971) The trouble with this view is that traditionally,

47

metaphysicians have argued that in order for something to be real, it must at least cause something to happen. Unfortunately, Dennett has no account of causation and has little patience with the metaphysical arguments that eliminativist philosophers deploy. Instead, Dennett maintains what he calls a *stance dependent realism* towards higher-level properties and objects. In order to understand how this approach avoids the metaphysical dilemma posed by the eliminativists we need to return once again to our chess computer.

The Intentional Stance

In practice, any half-decent chess-playing computer is too complicated to be easily predicted from either the design or physical stances. While the physical stance holds out the possibility of prediction and control in principle, physics alone is unlikely to provide the kind of help we'll need in defeating the machine at chess. In competition with a good chess computer, we will instinctively treat it as though it had beliefs and desires and was rational. To do so, is to adopt the intentional stance towards the computer.

It might seem inappropriate to say that I won't move my pawn because I can see that the computer *wants* me to leave my bishop unprotected. However, according to Dennett we should not be so quick to dismiss such talk. "The decision to adopt the strategy," according to Dennett, "is not intrinsically right or wrong. One can always refuse to adopt the intentional stance toward the computer, and accept its checkmates" (BR, 7) However, we will have reason to adopt the intentional stance "whenever we have reason to suppose the assumption of optimal design is warranted, and doubt the practicality of prediction from the design, or physical stance." (BR, 9) Optimal design, we'll recall is the property of certain organisms and machines whereby, in the case of the organism, we say that it has evolved to respond to the environment in a biologically appropriate fashion. In the case of a machine, the optimal design assumption is simply the idea that the programmer who engineered the system in question did a good job.

I should note that Dennett's discussion of the chess computer is not meant to imply that the chess computer is an adequate model of the mind, or that we adopt the same strategies toward a chess computer that we would toward another person:

> All that has been claimed is that on occasion a purely physical
> system can be so complex, and yet so organized, that we find
> it convenient, explanatory, pragmatically necessary for

> prediction to treat it as if it had beliefs and desires and was
> rational (BR, 7-8)

And yet, to agree that it is sensible, on pragmatic grounds, to treat certain kinds of things as though they had beliefs and desires seems to leave many of the most important questions in the philosophy of mind untouched. Traditional philosophers will point out that we are inevitably led into the metaphysical problem of distinguishing between those things that *really* have minds and those things that don't. Does the dog have beliefs? Does the snail?

Dennett's philosophy manages to tackle this boundary dispute in a rather indirect fashion. Rather than drawing a line too quickly around the kinds of things that can have beliefs and desires, Dennett introduces the neutral term *intentional system*. Things that are usefully treated as though they had minds belong to the class of intentional systems. Clearly we would normally count people, some other animals and a few machines as intentional systems. However, for Dennett an intentional system is anything "whose behavior can be (at least sometimes) explained and predicted by relying on ascriptions to the system of beliefs and desires." (BBS 495) When it comes to the boundary dispute over the kinds of things that have minds, it is much easier to determine whether a machine or an organism falls under the description of an intentional system that he presents than to solve the metaphysical problem of whether, for example, it really sees blue the way I do, whether it has a soul etc.

> The concept of an intentional system is a relatively uncluttered
> and unmetaphysical notion, abstracted as it is from questions
> of the constitution, composition, consciousness, morality or
> divinity of the objects falling under it. (BR, 12)

What Dennett has done with the notion of an intentional system is to offer a set of criteria, along Rylean lines, for mentality *per se*. Anything which fits the very general set of criteria for being an intentional system *is* an intentional system. Or, as Dennett is fond of saying: "handsome is as handsome does." Fixing on a set of criteria for distinguishing thinking from non-thinking things has proven incredibly difficult. Consequently, for most philosophers, his approach is disarmingly simple. Dennett's account of what it means to be an intentional system provides a purely pragmatic approach to the question. If it's useful to treat something as an intentional system, then it's an intentional system. The immediate philosophical temptation is to look behind mere pragmatic considerations to the nature of the device or organism in question. From Dennett's perspective, this temptation leads us down a dead end.

A useful way to think about the issue of deciding whether something is, or is not a member of the set of thinkers was proposed by Alan Turing. (1950) The famous Turing test doesn't rely on knowing what the object or person in question has in its brain or mind. In this sense it is an anticipation of Dennett's "handsome is as handsome does" approach to intentional systems. According to Turing a computer or anything else for that matter, qualifies as a thinking thing if it can regularly beat a human opponent in what he calls "the imitation game." The two players in the imitation game, the computer and the human, are hidden from view of the judges. Judges are permitted to ask any question of the two players and the players are permitted to respond in whatever way they wish. The object of the game is for the contestants to convince the judges that they are thinking and feeling things. In order to maintain anonymity, typed answers are presented to the judges from both players. The judges must then try to pick the human being based solely on these typed answers. If the judges fail to regularly identify the human contestant correctly, the computer must be allowed into our community of thinkers. As it turns out, Turing's test is incredibly difficult for a computer to pass. After all, judges are free to ask the contestants *any* question. No machine currently exists (and none is on the horizon) that can know enough and, more importantly, none can use its knowledge in a sufficiently flexible and socially appropriate manner to regularly pass the test. Turing's test, like Dennett's intentional systems approach relies solely on the behavior of the system. Dennett's intentional systems approach picks intentional systems on purely pragmatic grounds, Turing's test sets the standard for determining the kind of thing that can pass into the human community as full-fledged thinkers.

From the perspective of traditional philosophical inquiry into these matters, Dennett's intentional systems approach simply avoids the important issue. Many critics have insisted that the pragmatic or behavioral approach can't capture the distinctive intrinsic properties that divide thinkers from non-thinkers. In response, Dennett would insist that he has presented a new kind of realism, free from the crippling flaws inherent in older versions of realism; he calls it a *stance dependent realism*. If it walks like an intentional system and talks, barks or quacks like an intentional system then it's an intentional system. What the entity in question looks like, or is made of, is irrelevant to the determination of whether it can legitimately count as a

50

thinker. Like Turing, Dennett's account of what it is to be an intentional system is focused on the behavioral criteria that allow interpreters to pick out intentional systems. So, rather than focusing on some internal or essential property that all intentional systems possess, Dennett recognizes that we decide on what is to counts as an intentional system by reference to the functions or behaviors of the object in question. In this sense his view is thoroughly functionalist. In a recent paper he describes this kind of approach as:

> so ubiquitous in science that it is tantamount to a reigning presumption of all of science... The trajectory of cannonballs of equal mass and density is not affected by whether they are made of iron, copper or gold. It *might* have mattered, one imagines, but in fact it doesn't. And wings don't *have* to have feathers on them in order to power flight, and eyes don't have to be blue or brown in order to see. [...] it is science's job to find the maximally general, maximally non-committal–hence minimal–characterization of whatever power or capacity is under consideration. (unpublished ms., 9)

Dennett regards the intentional systems approach as providing a simple and maximally general set of criteria for drawing the line between thinkers and non-thinkers. So, for example, whatever else a person might be, he is an intentional system and whatever follows from being an intentional system also holds for people.

The first point that critics notice about Dennett's characterization of intentional systems is that something will only count as an intentional system in relation to the strategies of an interpreter who is trying to explain and predict its behavior. It is often pointed out that almost anything can be labeled an intentional system so long as it is treated as such by an interpreter. This point would seem to undermine Dennett's approach and has formed the core of most criticisms of his philosophy.

Objections to the Intentional Stance Approach 1: Nozick's Fancy Thermostat Argument

There have been numerous objections to what some see as Dennett's excessively liberal characterization of intentional systems. So, for example, while we would not normally treat things like thermostats or vending machines as having hopes, beliefs, desires and the like, perhaps, under certain circumstances it would be useful for someone to assume that the vending machine really *recognizes*, or fails to *recognize* the authenticity of my dollar bill. Or, conceivably I could interpret my thermostat as *believing* that the temperature is too low, that it *desires* the temperature to be 71 degrees Farenheidt and that it *acts* in accordance with these *beliefs* and *desires* to cause the furnace in my basement to begin heating the house. Should we then say that the thermostat and the vending machine are members of the class of intentional systems?

The behavior of thermostats and vending machines is easily explained without reference to beliefs and desires once we understand their design, and the physical principles underlying their function. However, this doesn't let Dennett off the hook. While we are smart enough to see thermostats and vending machines as explicable in terms of terms of their designs or in terms of their physical composition, the problem remains that shifting the perspective of the interpreter seems to change the judgment as to whether or not something counts as an intentional system. Some artifact, creature or person could be considered an intentional system from the point of view of one observer and not an intentional system from the point of view of another, observer? Surely we wouldn't want a situation where the status of an intentional system would change depending on whoever happens to be around at the time.

Criticizing Dennett, the philosopher Robert Nozick (1981) suggests that, in principle, some race of super intelligent aliens, could come to understand us solely in terms of the physiological processes that determine our actions and that they could thereby understand us without ever making reference to the intentional stance.

According to Dennett, while these super-intelligent aliens might, in principle correctly predict a person's actions one at a time through a meticulous study of his body and environment, this kind of prediction would be severely limited. It would focus on predictions of the behavior of individuals on a case-by-case basis. Contrast the laborious process involved in the alien's predictions with our own methods of predicting human behavior. Treating the person as an intentional system allows us non-aliens to rapidly predict his or her behavior in a wide variety of circumstances with relative ease. In short, the aliens, with their case-by-case predictions of action through a study of the physical constitution of the human body in its environment at a particular point in time would be missing the patterns of behavior in human life that we can easily capture from the intentional stance.

52

If the aliens asked us how we manage to predict one another so reliably without any real understanding of the physiological underpinnings of behavior we would tell a story something like the following: First you decide to treat the system in question as a rational agent; then you figure out what kinds of beliefs the agent ought to have given its place in the world and the kinds of things that are likely to interest it. You determine its desires based on the same considerations and knowing these you try to determine the course of action the system will take to achieve its desired outcome. Some practical reasoning will allow you to see what the agent ought to do, and on this basis you can reliably predict what it will do.

We would admit to the puzzled aliens that our method is "not good at predicting the events in fine-grain, but it does end up describing an arc of causation." (IS, 28) Our approach is a reliable rough and ready guide to human behavior. All things being equal, for example, we can be sure that if interest rates are lowered, then the Dow Jones Index will rise. We won't be able to predict the response of every stock with precision, but we'll almost certainly be able to predict the general trend of the index under these circumstances. And while we won't be able to predict the exact words or the cadence of his voice, most Americans will have a rough idea of the kinds of thing that a Republican or Democratic candidate for President of the United States would say in response to a question about the legal status of abortion. From the perspective of our super-intelligent aliens, this predictive power would be nothing short of miraculous if they didn't appreciate our use of the intentional stance.

So, according to Dennett, the intentional systems approach reveals patterns that are not available to the design or the physical stances. And while his analysis of the intentional stance takes its starting point with the observer, it's not all in the eye of the beholder, there are still questions of right and wrong in the determination of what is to count as an intentional system. As Dennett puts it: "The decision to adopt the intentional stance is free, but the facts about the success or failure of the stance, were one to adopt it, are perfectly objective." (24)

Dennett's views on intentionality and the intentional stance have changed slightly over the twenty or so years from their early form in *Content and Consciousness* and 'Intentional Systems' to the shape they took in his 1987 collection of essays *The Intentional Stance*. Over the years the instrumentalist tone of 'Intentional Systems' has softened considerably in response to the kinds of criticism raised by philosophers like Nozick.

Objections to the Intentional Stance Approach 2: Dennett's Interpretationism Misses the Inner Mechanisms

Fodor, Dretske, Jacob and others criticize Dennett's argument that folk psychology is best understood as tool for prediction of future behavior and that its terms ('belief', 'desire' and the like) must be understood by reference to the strategy of the interpreter. They call Dennett's view *interpretationism*. Against Dennett, these philosophers insist on the reality of human beliefs and desires as inner causes of behavior. Surely, they argue, if folk psychology proves so useful, it must be because it's making reference to real things taking place in the mind/brain of the person or animal in question. Folk psychology, according to these thinkers, reveals the inner causes of behavior.

The most popular inner-cause theory in the philosophy of mind is Jerry Fodor's 'language-of-thought' hypothesis. (see Fodor 1975) While this view of the mind has had considerable influence in cognitive psychology, it rests on the dubious philosophical presupposition that our folk psychological statements must make reference to inner causes in order for them to be true. For philosophers like Fodor if it is true that "Jane voted for Nader because she believed him to be the best candidate" then it must be true that a belief "Nader is the best candidate" caused her action. If Fodor's language of thought hypothesis is correct, then the brain, which controls Jane's bodily movements is governed by processes that are, in turn, governed by language-like (syntactically structured) representations. Fodor argues that the belief must exist in Jane's brain in such a way that it can simultaneously cause the actions that constitute voting *and* interact with other representations in a reasonable way. Her beliefs must be organized and interact in the same way in the brain as they do in our commonsense reasoning. The representation of her belief "Nader is the best candidate" must exist in Jane's brain in such a way as to make it compatible with certain other representations such as "Nader is a candidate", "There can only be one best candidate", etc. Furthermore, it must exist in such a way as to make it incompatible with the belief that Bush or Gore are better candidates than Nader

For Fodor our ordinary folk psychological generalizations and habits not only provide a useful way to predict the behavior of our fellows, but offer a source of scientific insight into the inner workings of the mind/brain. The assumption underlying Fodor's philosophical reflection is the belief that, in order for folk psychological statements to be true, they must be statements about the inner causes of our actions.

54

Dennett argues that it is an unwarranted philosophical step to go from the truthfulness of folk-psychological statements to the idea that those statements are uncovering some kind of inner mechanism.

The inner cause thesis has a number of important weaknesses that make it very unlikely that it will ever become a legitimate part of the brain and behavioral sciences. Like most philosophers Dennett thinks it extremely improbable that neuroscience will uncover distinguishable mechanisms that would be possessed by everyone sharing a particular belief. For example, as we shall see below, it is almost impossible to imagine the kind of internal mechanism that would be at work in *all* instances of such phenomena as wanting a sandwich or believing that Australia is a continent. This presents a significant barrier to the kinds of future discoveries that the inner-cause thesis presupposes. It would lead us to doubt, for example, whether we will ever discover the kinds of language-like representations that Fodor assumes must exist.

Contra Fodor, one could argue that the intentional stance is so useful and so widely applicable that its very generality makes it almost certain to fail to pick out any mechanisms or processes that are unique to one species or another. We use the intentional stance with considerable success when talking about everything from chess computers to birds to people. So, while the intentional stance may be useful and may even generate objectively true statements, this does not necessarily license us to imply that it is a fruitful guide to the mechanisms at work in human brain. Take, for example the following statements that arise from the perspective of the intentional stance:

(a) The only reason Fido is obeying you is because he *wants* a biscuit.
(b) I won't move my pawn because I can see that the computer *wants* me to leave my rook unprotected
(c) She buys lottery tickets because she *thinks* she has a chance to win.

Let's return, for a moment to the problem that arises when we call these statements true. What makes statements like (a) - (c) true or false? Is it true that the chess computer *wants* me to leave my pawn unprotected? In some obvious sense, the answer is yes. However, one might doubt whether the chess computer wants to win in the same way that the dog wants a biscuit? And surely the computer and the dog *want* in a way that differs again from the way the person in (c) *wants* to win the lottery. As we shall see, Dennett's intentional stance account goes against the grain of questions like these, asking us instead to focus on the function of words like 'want' from the perspective of the strategist who utters them. This way of looking at the words we use to talk about minds leads him to claim that, in some sense the word 'want' in (a) - (c) is basically playing an equivalent role in each sentence.

Most traditional philosophers would insist that the word 'want' in (a) - (c) refers to different things in each of the three instances. Some might say, for instance, that the computer doesn't really want anything, that it's just a machine that carries out the instructions coded into its software, or that there is such a fundamental difference between the way animals and humans experience desire that it makes no sense to think of the 'want' in (a) and (c) as referring to the same kind of thing.

If we follow traditional philosophers down this path, the alleged differences tempt us into thinking that we can consider the minds under consideration 'from the inside'. Surely there is something about being a dog that is so different from being a computer that it makes no sense to think of them as desiring in the same way? We empathize with our pets and, in our weaker moments, we think we can imagine life from the perspective of our dogs. We imagine that being a dog would be some version of ourselves but much cruder and more immediately bodily - lots of grunting, scratching and desiring but not much reflection. And if it's like anything to be a computer, we might imagine, it's probably very peaceful and quiet.

This kind of reflection is a prosaic version of the rarified philosophical practice known as phenomenology. Dennett will argue that, for scientific purposes at least, such lines of investigation are often a waste of time and that they can often be highly misleading. While traditional philosophers might urge us to dig deeper into the minds of the creatures in (a) - (c), Dennett urges us to look first to the stance of the beholder. What (a) - (c) share in common is *not* that they all refer to some fundamental internal state corresponding to desire. It is highly unlikely that an examination of the innards of the three *wanters* would reveal some physical structure corresponding to their wants that they shared in common. Furthermore, even if there was some physical structure shared in common, it is almost certain that we could find a fourth *wanter* who wouldn't have it.

So, although we should not necessarily exclude the existence of neural patterns or structures that are common to animals that 'want', these structures are generally irrelevant, according to Dennett, to the kinds of claims we make about other minds. Instead, (a) - (c) are all instances of reports from the intentional stance, they are all shorthand accounts of the predictive strategies that their speakers and hearers have adopted towards the world. Some instances of the intentional strategy manage to successfully allow us to predict the future behavior of a system, some don't.

56

For Dennett, one can be right about someone's beliefs or desires in the same way one can be right about whether someone would make a good husband or a good mayor. For example, I believe that my friend Marie would make a great mayor. In my judgment, her character and abilities suit her for the position and bode well for great success in public office. However, saying this does not imply the existence of something like a good mayor gene in her DNA or an essence of *good mayorness* in Marie's soul. I am simply predicting that, given the right opportunities and the right circumstances, Marie would perform very well as mayor. Similarly, when we say that someone or something wants or believes something, the truth of our claim is not a matter of correctly locating, or picking out some internal structure in the person's brain or mind. Instead, our ascriptions of belief and desire are, for the most part, reports on the strategy we are using to predict that person's behavior. If we have adopted a good strategy for predicting the behavior of the person or animal in question, then we have at least some reason to call our statements about that person's state true.

Moderate Realism and the Problem of Justification

Critics have focused on what they see as Dennett's denial that various aspects of mental life truly exist and as we have seen, he is famous for being a toughly skeptical critic of those who (like Fodor) believe that such psychological objects *must* certainly exist in the way electrons or planets exist, solely by virtue of the fact that we really need to talk about them to get by in ordinary life. While Dennett has certainly been a vocal critic of realists like Fodor and Dretske it would be a mistake to infer from this criticism that he is an eliminativist. Dennett is often read this way. Take for instance Jerry Fodor and Ernest LePore's presentation of Dennett's views in their 'Is Intentional Ascription Intrinsically Normative.' (DAC, 70-82) In that paper, they cite a passage from *The Intentional Stance* where Dennett says that "[s]trictly speaking, ontologically speaking, there are no such things as beliefs, desires or other intentional phenomena." (IS, 342) While this looks like a straightforward statement of eliminativism, it should be read in its original context. The citation comes from a passage where Dennett is describing the aftermath of Quine's analysis of the propositional attitudes. For Quine,

> If we are limning the true and ultimate structure of reality, the canonical scheme for us is the austere scheme that knows

no quotation but direct quotation and no prepositional attitudes but only the physical constitution and behavior of organisms (WO, 221 as cited in IS, 342)

And, as we saw in Chapter Three, eliminativist conclusions inevitably follow from strict Quinean premises. In response to these Quinean consequences, Dennett notes that we are still left having to use the intentional idiom in daily life. This is the case even though we can make no sense of the kinds of reduction of psychological discourse to physical discourse that some had hoped for.

> The intentional idioms are "practically indispensable," and we should see what we can do to make sense of their employment in what Quine called an "essentially dramatic" idiom (p.219). Not just brute facts, then, but an element of interpretation, and dramatic interpretation at that, must be recognized in any use of the intentional vocabulary (IS, 342)

We can still use the intentional idiom, according to Dennett, just as long as we recognize that we can never separate its use from the fallible context of interpretation. Quine's lesson, according to Dennett, is that there are no final *facts of the* matter when it comes to meaning. For Dennett, this element of interpretation has been widely recognized by his colleagues in the philosophy of mind. And, he argues, almost all of the strenuous debates since Quine have been about "how to play this dramatic interpretation game."(IS, 342) Dennett makes a significant historical point when he writes:

> Here we find Quine and Sellars in fundamental agreement about the not-purely-descriptive nature of intentional attribution, and just about everyone since has concurred, though with different emphases. Most for instance have thought Quine's claim that these idioms are merely practically indispensable underestimated the centrality of the role they play – but if we took out the "merely" there might be little left to debate. (IS, 342)

The important point to draw from Dennett's reflection on these debates is that he doesn't see his work as being continuous with traditional worries about the ontological status of mental entities. This position stands in sharp contrast with that of realists like Fodor. Fodor has insisted that intentional states must be irreducible, real *and* accessible to the physical sciences. One way of achieving these three goals is by grounding intentional states in the syntax of representations (as described above, in the discussion of inner causes). As we have seen, this approach faces profound difficulties. However, for realists like Fodor and LePore, there must be a matter of fact as to whether or not a certain intentional ascription is true. If I believe that Neil Armstrong walked on the moon, then, for the realist, this is a fact with just as much right to facthood as the fact that Neil Armstrong walked on the moon.

There is something intuitively appealing about the realist position. However, if we follow Dennett in accepting Quinean lessons with respect to prepositional attitudes we will have to give up the search for hard and fast facts about beliefs and desires. In his account of the intentional stance and particularly in the passages in question Dennett is describing the ways we play the dramatic interpretation game. After Quine, according to Dennett, philosophers should not be trying to provide a recipe for uncovering the facts about belief. Instead, for Dennett the point is to determine the ways that notions like belief emerge from the process of interpretation. For Dennett, predicting the behavior of other animals is a practical problem that has been solved in a variety of ways by organisms over the course of natural history. The intentional idiom is part of our bag of tools for predicting the behavior of other animals. It is not a metaphysical matter to be settled once and for all.

Realists insist that there must be some fact of the matter that makes our intentional ascriptions true or false (successful or unsuccessful). Dennett, and other like him, deny the relevance of the realists' putative *facts of the matter* focusing instead on the practical business of ascribing beliefs and desires to organisms. How do we, in practice, interpret the beliefs and desires of others? We have already touched on one common strategy that Dennett outlines in his account of the intentional stance. Intentional ascriptions involve attributing "to a creature the prepositional attitudes it "ought to have" given its circumstances." (IS, 342) Guidelines that allow us to determine what an organism *ought* to believe are sometimes called *normative principles*.

The projective approach, on the other hand, (sometimes called the principle of humanity (Grandy, 1973)) involves the interpreter's imagining himself in the place of the person or animal he hopes to understand. So, if I hear Anne say "I don't think there are any cookies left," according to the projectivist strategy, I come to understand her by imagining myself uttering the same sentence. This would probably lead me to think something like "Anne is in the state that would normally cause me to say 'I don't think there are any cookies left'" (for a more detailed discussion of projectivism and its drawbacks see Fodor and LePore in DAC, 71f).

Fodor and LePore correctly demonstrate that neither projectivism nor nomativism can serve as indubitable ways of justifying an interpreter's judgments with respect to the beliefs and desires of other people and animals. But unfortunately, for the kinds of arguments that Fodor and LePore want to mount against Dennett, he has never argued that projectivism and nomativism are theories that allow us to, for example, determine the precise reference of sentences about belief and desire. Instead, the projective and normative approaches are simply ways that we manage to generate interpretations in the dramatic interpretation game. For Dennett, it is a mistake to see these two theories of dramatic interpretation; 'projectivism' and 'nomativism' as providing a foolproof and certain justification for judgments concerning concepts. Instead, the normative approach and the projectivist approach merge into one another as part of the rough and ready cluster of practices we use in our effort to try and understand one another.

Fodor and LePore attack Dennett's claim that all statements about mental life contain an element of interpretation by attempting to show that it rests on shaky foundations.

> Dennett's view depends on showing that Normativism or Projectivism (or both) are true; but since Projectivism is hopeless, the argument depends *de facto* on Normativism being true. (DAC, 80)

While they are certainly important components in Dennett's philosophy the Projective Principle and the Normative Principle (described below) do not play the kind of justificatory function in Dennett's thought that Fodor and LePore assume every good philosophical theory calls for.

For Dennett, when we try to understand mental life we have no choice but to begin *in medias res*. Similarly, in the science of mind, we cannot start from an indubitable set of truths or intuitions. So, while we must assume that most of our scientific heritage is reasonably reliable, we recognize that human understanding, especially our attempts to understand one another are fallible and subject to revision.

Dennett (1991) insists that he is a "moderate" realist with respect to the terms of folk psychology. He believes that the patterns we discover in the behavior and behavioral dispositions of a system are objectively real. However, this is a *moderate* realism in the following

60

respect: If there are two or more adequate but different systems of intentional ascriptions (two sets of beliefs and desires) that can be ascribed in a useful way to an individual, Dennett believes that there is *no fact of the matter* about which of the two *really* applies to that system. (1987b, 1991) This echoes the kind of indeterminacy that Quine pointed to in his 1960. Quine demonstrates that an anthropologist with two different translation manuals, both of which allow him to get by smoothly in an alien language community, has no way of deciding which of the two *truly* applies to the alien language. Of course, Quine would never take his thesis of the indeterminacy of translation as denying of the possibility of translation *per se*. Nor is it a denial that, in practice, some translations work better than others. We can all agree that there is good translation and bad translation and better translation and worse translation, and that in general we can agree on rankings of pairs of translations. Now the question is, what if there was a "tie for first place" between two candidates that were non-trivially different from each other? Would it have to be resolvable? Quine and Dennett would say no; there could be no fact of the matter that showed why one had to be better, and yet it could be clear that both were hugely superior to the next best translation. Anyone who insists that this is impossible, that one of the translations has to be better is, in Dennett's terms, a hysterical realist.

Quine's point with the example of the two equivalent translation manuals is that our evaluation of translations relies on pragmatic and behavioral criteria alone. There are no intrinsic properties of the foreign language that one of the two imaginary translation manuals more closely approximates.

Similarly, Dennett would insist that our judgments on matters of belief and desire can't be settled by reference to some intrinsic property of the mind or brain in question. This does not mean that objective accounts of mental life are impossible. Like the Quinean translator we have ordinary, fallible, ways of judging the truthfulness of statements about the mental lives of others and like the Quinean translator, we have no evidence for the suitability of our judgments aside from pragmatic and behavioral considerations.

This attitude towards issues like folk psychology, translation and the like, stands in stark contrast with much of the philosophical tradition. In the past, philosophers followed Descartes in believing that our self-knowledge; the certainty of our own existence as thinking things, could serve as an indubitable foundation for science and could function as a standard against which we could evaluate the truth of all other judgments. While certain parts of the natural world might remain difficult for us to know with certainty, philosophers believed that one thing everyone could know for sure was his or her own mind. Naturalists like Dennett have helped cause a fundamental shift in the way philosophers view our knowledge of mental life.

For reasons described in Chapter Three philosophers no longer treat our everyday intuitions about thoughts as self-evident data for philosophical reflection. We do not assume, for instance that the brain works in the same way that our ordinary commonsense reasoning about beliefs and desires might lead us to assume. Instead, thanks in large part to Dennett's work, philosophers and scientists have become interested in understanding how the mind emerges from a biological and social context. However, since it is so difficult to imagine doing without folk psychology, we are faced with the new philosophical problem of explaining why our talk of beliefs and desires serves us so well in ordinary life. Dennett describes this shift in perspective as follows:

> Until recently... philosophers (and other theorists) have tended to endow our everyday intuitions about our minds with an invulnerable certainty or incontrovertibility. This invulnerable status must be denied to the putative truths of folk psychology, while at the same time we acknowledge the very great powers of organization and expectation we derive from it. The task that lies ahead is to describe accurately and then explain the power of folk psychology. (BBS 496)

So, rather than taking our everyday intuitions about the mind as a foundation for philosophical theories, we are now engaged in the process of trying to understand the reasons behind the usefulness of folk psychology. The intentional stance provides a way of understanding how the words we use to talk about the mind serve such a central function in the prediction and explanation of behavior. For example, just as Edward Tolman's 'mental maps' serve to organize the experimental data revealed by his studies of memory in the rat, the folk psychologist relies on theoretical constructs that allow him to project a virtual world of beliefs and desires onto the behavior of others. Dennett sees scientific and philosophical investigations of the mind as providing an explanation of why these theoretical constructs can work as well as they do.

Surely there is no way to reduce our conscious experience; our pains, tickles, sense of self, imagination, pride and desire to the virtual projection or the theoretical construction of an interpreter? Our unshakeable faith in the reality of consciousness poses the greatest obstacle to Dennett's way of thinking about the mind. However, perhaps our confidence with regard to consciousness is misplaced. In his extraordinary little book *Studies in Words* (1960) C.S. Lewis reminds us how strange words like 'conscious' can appear in the work of familiar authors from the relatively recent past. He considers, for example, the use of the word 'conscious' in Jane Austen:

> In *Northanger Abbey* (ch. xxx) Henry Tilney is introduced to Mrs. Morland 'by her conscious daughter'. She was *conscious* in exactly this classical sense; knowing much which her mother did not know about Henry and her own relations to him, she was in a secret, shared a knowledge with him.

The meaning of *conscious* as Austen uses it, shares an etymological connection with our more modern notion of consciousness, but on the surface at least 'conscious' functions quite differently in Austen's text. For us, *consciousness* refers to something like the state of mind that most of us experience when we are not asleep. In Austen's time, there would have been nothing strange about Mrs. Jennings of *Sense and Sensibility* believing that Colonel Brandon's letter had something to do with Miss Williams 'because' as she said 'he looked so conscious when I mentioned her.' (ch.xiv) In the chapter that follows, we will examine Dennett's account of consciousness in light of the realism/anti-realism issues that have occupied us in this chapter.

5

Consciousness

By the mid-1960s Dennett saw that exciting times were ahead for anyone interested in knowing how the brain does the mind's work. While he recognized that developments in neuroscience and cognitive science held important implications for a number of traditional philosophical problems, he had to argue vigorously for the legitimacy of a scientifically-informed approach to the philosophy of mind. It is important to recognize that for much of the twentieth century mainstream scientists had deliberately avoided a number of basic problems in the philosophy of mind. In particular, the so-called mind-body problem, which had plagued modern philosophy for centuries was widely ignored by mainstream scientists.

Perhaps the most difficult part of the mind-body problem is the problem of understanding how living physical bodies in the physical world can give rise to consciousness. How can a physical object like a human or animal brain be the conscious subject of experience? How can a brain be a thinker, a deliberator, or a sufferer of pain? With the development of modern neuroscience, we are beginning to get some grasp on the underlying mechanisms that will eventually allow us to answer questions like this. However, even if we knew *everything* about the anatomy and biochemical processes in the brain and central nervous system, we wouldn't necessarily know *anything* about the mind. Connecting what we know about the brain with what we think we know about the mind requires us to move beyond the confines of neuroanatomy and neurophysiology into the somewhat murkier regions

64

of the philosophy of mind. One of Dennett's great contributions to the study of mental life has been his ability to bring philosophy and science together. His first step was to convince scientists that traditional philosophical problems, like the problem of consciousness are worth investigating. So, for example, even as late as 1987, Dennett teased the scientific community into recognizing that it was possible to talk sensibly about the mind:

> Talking about the mind, for many people, is rather like talking about sex: slightly embarrassing, undignified, maybe even disreputable. "Of course it exists," some might say, "but do we have to talk about it?" Yes, we do. Many people would rather talk about the brain (which, after all, *is* the mind) and would like to think that all the wonderful things we need to say about people could be said without lapsing into vulgar, undisciplined *mentalistic* talk. (IS, 1)

Scientists were suspicious of mentalistic talk, in part because it seemed as though acknowledging the existence of mental life led to intractable philosophical problems. From the perspective of modern scientists, philosophers had struggled to settle the mind-body problem for centuries with no real success and little evidence of progress. As a result, until relatively recently, wary scientists were happy to leave the whole embarrassing topic to philosophers. In his important 1978 paper 'Towards a Cognitive Theory of Consciousness,' Dennett noted that cognitive scientists had paid almost no attention to consciousness:

> [O]ne finds not so much a lack of interest as a deliberate avoidance of the issue. I think I know why. Consciousness appears to be the last bastion of occult properties, epiphenomena, immeasurable subjective states – in short, the one area of mind best left to the philosophers, who are welcome to it. Let them make fools of themselves trying to corral the quicksilver of "phenomenology" into a respectable theory. (BR, 149)

It is impossible to deny that we are conscious and yet, it seems difficult to imagine the kind of explanation that would allow science to make sense of this very private, and yet undeniably real phenomenon. Consciousness has long been a source of bafflement and wonder for philosophers. Imagine tasting whiskey, smelling cheese, feeling a tickle or a sharp pain in the knee. In each of these cases one experiences a very different kind of feeling. But what are these experiences? And how could they possibly arise out of the action of the brain and nervous system?

When we think of consciousness, we tend to think of it "from the inside", from privacy of our own perspective. However, proper science demands that our claims be open for public confirmation. In *The Intentional Stance* Dennett writes: 'I propose to see [...] just what the mind looks like from the third person, materialistic perspective of contemporary science.' (IS, 7) However, given the intensely private quality of consciousness, many thinkers have doubted whether this third-person perspective can really convey the nature of this important aspect of mental life.

In their quest for objectivity, natural scientists have long eschewed personal biases and subjective impressions in favor of objective and measurable evidence. Consequently, Dennett's project faces the problem of doing 'justice to the most private and ineffable subjective experiences, while never abandoning the methodological scruples of science.' (CE 72) Many philosophers believe that this third-person perspective necessarily excludes the essentially private, or first-person aspects of human life and therefore misses *what it's like* to be conscious.

Early in the history of modern science, subjective aspects of experience – phenomena such as the way a particular color looks to me, or the way I feel when I hear a piece of music – experiences that were difficult to quantify or explicitly share with others, were systematically excluded from science. Philosophers like Thomas Nagel, Charles Taylor and others have claimed that science will always be unable to explain mental life, and especially consciousness in any meaningful way. For Nagel, certain aspects of conscious experience will forever remain beyond the limits of scientific investigation. In his most famous article, Nagel argued that no matter how much we know about bat brains and bat behavior, no scientific explanation can tell us *what it's like* to be a bat. (Nagel 1974) The challenge then, is to understand how Dennett's third-person perspective can approach what we intuitively think of as the most private aspects of experience.

In one of its senses, "conscious" is simply synonymous with "awake." Being awake is a relatively *public* property of people and other animals. However, most philosophers have followed Nagel in arguing that consciousness is the most *private* thing in the world. Only the person himself or herself has privileged knowledge of his or her conscious experience. Even if someone were to tell us, in exhaustive detail, what she believed absinthe tastes like or what it's like to go bungee jumping, her account would still leave out the essentially private quality of her experiences.

In the mid-seventies, in response to the pessimism expressed by philosophers like Nagel, Dennett began to outline an empirical approach to human consciousness. There are two major components to his approach: On the one hand Dennett offers an hypothesis with respect to the neural mechanisms that give rise to experience. This *subpersonal* theory describes the kinds of processes that might plausibly be shown to be at work in the brain of the conscious person. On the other hand he has an account of the means by which we can come to understand "what it is like" to be another person or animal. He calls this approach *heterophenomenology*. While the term might seem to invoke some extremely technical or obscure practice, most of us are already experienced heterophenomenologists. As we shall see, the heterophenomenological method promises a way of reconciling objective scientific inquiry with the kind of private experience that Nagel believed lay beyond the limits of scientific inquiry.

A method for learning what it's like: heterophenomenology

When investigating consciousness, the best way to begin, according to Dennett, is by saying nothing at all about what consciousness might actually be. This simple starting point is already a radical step, given that most philosophers of mind since Descartes begin with the assumption that consciousness is something we know very well indeed. For Descartes, our self-knowledge as thinking things is so secure that it can serve as the foundation for all knowledge. Nevertheless, Dennett shakes off the tradition by asking philosophers and scientists to assume nothing about consciousness from the outset. The most obvious advantage of this approach is that it avoids introducing metaphysical objects of various kinds into the investigation prematurely and, of course, it prevents us from being discouraged by the apparently insurmountable privacy barrier that Nagel has described.

So, if we are interested in the scientific study of human consciousness, where do we begin? In practical terms, any ethical investigation of people involves the use of language. We assume, for instance that the subject involved in the experiment understands the instructions that the experimenter has presented, that he or she has agreed to participate in the experiment etc. In this context the initial stage in any study of consciousness will involve focusing on the record of what the experimental subjects and the experimentalists say during the experiment. This record constitutes a text that the investigator must later sit down and interpret.

Interpreting a text like this requires that the investigator make a number of working assumptions. He or she will almost certainly assume that the text is the "product of a process that has an intentional interpretation" i.e., that the subject and the experimenter were not merely forcing strings of meaningless noises from their throats, but that the text consists "of things that the speakers *wanted* to say, of *propositions* they meant to *assert* for various *reasons*."(CE, 82). This, of course, is Dennett's famous intentional stance in action. The intentional stance is invaluable in any investigation of human cognitive performance, and yet, we should always be aware of the assumptions underlying this useful interpretive strategy. He describes the two major assumptions that are initially in play during the heterophenomenological investigation as follows:

(1) that the noises (and other conventional acts) produced by the subject are interpretable as text

(2) that their text is interpretable (defeasibly, and to a first approximation, as we shall see) as a sincere and reliable (error corrected) account of their current *beliefs* or *opinions* (1982, 163)

These initial assumptions are justified solely on pragmatic grounds. Skeptics may certainly challenge either assumption. However, it would be impossible to design experiments to test aspects of human cognition without assuming that the participants were rational, could understand language, that their utterances had some meaning, etc. "Whatever dangers we run by adopting the intentional stance towards these verbal behaviors," Dennett writes "they are the price we must pay for gaining access to a host of reliable truisms we exploit in the design of experiments." (CE 78) In response to the skeptic we could also point out that these are the risks we run in our ordinary dealings with human beings on a daily basis.

However, critics could ask, doesn't Dennett's use of the intentional stance at this stage of the heterophenomenological method assume that his subjects are conscious? Hasn't Dennett already assumed a great deal about human cognition in defiance of his stated aim of assuming nothing about consciousness? By assuming, for instance, when we meet the subject of our experiment for the first time, that he or she is conscious and rational, maybe we are missing an important divide in the human race between those of us who really have consciousness and those who do not. A skeptic could argue that we have no secure grounds for assuming that our interlocutor in an experiment is conscious. Any given human being might, for example, be a zombie; a creature that looks and behaves like the rest of us (a physical and behavioral replica) but without any conscious experience. Zombies, as philosophers are fond of saying, are a metaphysical possibility; it is logically possible that ordinary looking people could be living what look like ordinary lives in the complete absence of any conscious experience.

Zombies are a bit of an embarrassment for philosophers. The Zombie argument has been one of the main weapons in the arsenal of those who deny the possibility of an explanation of consciousness. However, as arguments go it strikes most scientists and non-philosophers as a preposterously weak. (Dennett, 1995) The main thrust of the argument is that no matter what level of physical description we might achieve, no matter how accurately we could capture the physical details of the brain and nervous system, it is always possible to imagine that the physical story takes place in the complete absence of consciousness. Philosophers like John Searle, David Chalmers, Colin McGinn, Joseph Levine and many others dismiss computational, mechanistic and biological models of consciousness on *zombic* grounds. It's always possible that these physical stories still leave out the residual conscious something, hence naturalist explanations are never going to be good enough. Dennett has called this widespread impulse the *Zombic Hunch*. (1999) 'We are all *susceptible* to the Zombic Hunch,' Dennett writes, 'but if we are to credit it, we need a good argument.' (1999, ms.10) It turns out that there are no good arguments for taking the Zombic Hunch seriously. (Dennett, 1995) The argument rests on the idea that a functionally identical replica of a conscious being might lack some intrinsic (non-functional) property that would leave it unconscious but otherwise indistinguishable from its conscious twin. The burden of proof lies with the proponent of the zombie argument. He must show what kind of property could make the crucial difference between the zombie and his conscious twin. Furthermore, this would have to be a property that did nothing and had no role in the brain and behavior of the conscious organism. It might be possible to imagine properties like this, but their conceivability hardly warrants our seriously questioning naturalist models of consciousness.

In any event, there is no reason for the heterophenomenologist to worry about the threat of zombies in his research since, to begin with, the data that are presented to our experimenter are drawn from a text, rather than a *person*. In the great tradition initiated by Alan Turing, he or she will focus, not on the subject's physical presence, or appearance, but on what he, she or it says or does. The heterophenomenomolgist will listen carefully to a subject's responses including his or her introspective reports, taking them as, more or less, sincere accounts of what the subject believes.

So, once we have this text before us, what's the next step? Like any text, reading requires interpretation. The kind of interpretation that the theorist must undertake is analogous to the way one might read a work of fiction. In the case of a fictional text, reading involves a kind of worldbuilding. When one reads a compelling novel, say for instance Joseph Conrad's *The Secret Agent* one slips easily into the world of its central characters. Readers come to know this world well enough that we can easily imagine answering questions about aspects of this world that were not explicitly mentioned in Conrad's text. We could wonder about the Professor's past, or about Winnie's relationship with Verloc etc. Certain kinds of claims about the world of the novel can be true or false within the context of the fictional world of the novel itself, others must be left indeterminate.

Dennett explicitly connects the process of interpretation involved in reading a fictional work with the heterophenomenological reading that the experimenter performs on the subject's text:

> The reader of a novel lets the text constitute a fictional world, a world constituted by fiat by the text, exhaustively extrapolated as far as extrapolation will go and indeterminate beyond; our experimenter, the heterophenomenologist, lets the subject's text constitute that subject's heterophenomenological world, a world determined by fiat by the text (as interpreted) and indeterminate beyond [...] The subject's heterophenomenological world will be a stable, intersubjectively confirmable theoretical posit, having the same metaphysical status as Sherlock Holmes's London or the world according to Garp (CE 81)

As we shall see, the analogy between a reader of fiction and the heterophenomenologist works to suggest a number of important points about human consciousness. However, it's also a little disconcerting to treat our portrait of the subject's consciousness as something with the same metaphysical status as 'Sherlock Holmes's London or the world according to Garp.' Hence, one initial objection to the heterophenomenological method is that it fails to make contact with the phenomena that the heterophenomenological text is *really* talking about. When the subject reports that he feels a pain, or that he hopes that the Red Sox will beat the Yankees, it seems reasonable to say that he is *really* talking about his pain or his hope. Unlike a work of fiction, the critic might object, when people say things about what goes on in their minds, they are talking about real, existing things. How then can Dennett's heterophenomenological strategy help us discover what the subject is really talking about?

This is where the analogy with literary fiction begins to pay off. As readers, we are free to interpret a work of fiction in a way that the author might find objectionable, or in a way that he had simply not noticed. For instance, if we have some knowledge of the author's life and we notice that the evil older woman character in the novel bears a striking resemblance to the author's mother, we might be led to reinterpret certain events or passages in the text. Whether or not the author intended this interpretation to be obvious or even if he was completely unaware of it, this insight could potentially provide us with access to something other than the statements contained in the raw uninterpreted text of the novel.

Interpreting the subject's text is by no means an arbitrary matter. An interpretation is subject to the ordinary standards we would use to confirm or deny the merit of any scientific hypothesis. For instance, our confidence in the interpretation would be reinforced if, for instance, the novelist's mother left a letter complaining about the depiction of the evil old woman in his story. Of course, evidence against our interpretation might also be uncovered. However, the main point to notice however is that the theorist's interpretation of the subject's text is an objective theoretical hypothesis that can be shared with others and is subject to confirmation and denial given suitable evidence. The method for investigating and describing phenomenology presented by Dennett involves extracting and purifying the subject's texts, and using those texts to generate a theoretical construct, the subject's heterophenomenological world, a world "populated with all the images, events, sounds, smells, hunches, presentiments, and feelings that the subject (apparently) sincerely believes to exist in his or her stream of consciousness." (CE 98)

Dennett treats the objects of heterophenomenological investigation as parts of a theoretical construct. This is precisely the difference between heterophenomenolgy and phenomenology as it is usually understood. According to the phenomenologist, the objects he investigates are *real* objects rather than theoretical hypotheses. Dennett

71

depicts the debate along the following lines. The phenomenologist protests that:

> When I tell you sincerely that I am imagining a purple cow, I am not just unconsciously producing a word string to that effect [...] cunningly contrived to coincide with some faintly analagous physical happenings in my brain; I am consciously and deliberately reporting the existence of something that is *really there!* It is no mere theorist's fiction to me. (CE, 97)

Dennett responds:

> Well, you *are* unconsciously producing a word-string; you haven't a clue to how you do that, or to what goes into its production. But you insist you are not *just* doing that; you know why you're doing it; you *understand* the word-string and *mean* it. I agree. That's why it works so well to constitute a heterophenomenological world. If you were just parroting words more of less at random, the odds against the sequence of words yielding such an interpretation would be astronomical. Surely there is a good explanation of how and why you say what you do, an explanation that accounts for the difference between just saying something and saying it and meaning it, but you don't have that explanation yet. At least not all of it... Probably you are talking about something real, at least most of the time. Let us see if we can find out what it is. (CE, 97)

In effect, according to Dennett, the heterophenomenological world constructed by the theorist is a portrait "of *what it is like to be* that subject – in the subject's own terms, given the best interpretation we can muster." (CE 98) Of course, philosophers like Nagel would object that Dennett's heterophenomenology can never really make contact with what it is that the subject's text is *really* about. However, Dennett's response would be that the subject him or herself probably has about the same, if not less of a firm grasp on the nature of the things that he or she believes populate her inner world than the theorist. Notice that in his response, Dennett cheekily enlists the phenomenologist himself into the project of trying to figure out what he thinks: "Probably you are talking about something real, at least most of the time. Let us see if *we* can find out what it is." (CE, 97)

My mind's playing tricks on me.

Like Ryle, Dennett questions the idea that we have some privileged knowledge of ourselves that resists the usual methods of scientific inquiry. When we come to know ourselves, according to Ryle, we do almost exactly what we do when we wish to know about other people and things.

> The sorts of things that I can find out about myself are the same as the sorts of things that I can find out about other people, and the methods of finding them out are much the same. A residual difference in the supplies of the requisite data makes some difference in degree between what I can know about myself and what I can know about you, but these differences are not all in favor of self-knowledge. (COM 155)

Dennett follows Ryle in believing that the difference between self-knowledge and our knowledge of other people and objects is a matter of degree rather than kind. However, in *Consciousness Explained*, Dennett goes even further, suggesting ways in which we could be mistaken about our own introspective reports. He argued that much of our self-description; our auto- (as opposed to hetero-) phenomenology may be little more than confabulation. To confabulate is to make up a story without 'realizing' it. There is considerable neuroscientific and psychological evidence showing that confabulation is an integral part of the way we think about ourselves.

Confabulation, to one extent or another, is part of normal psychology. Of course in extreme cases, confabulation must be considered a kind of memory disorder. Pathological cases of confabulation occasionally occur in patients with damage to the basal forebrain and the frontal lobes. Unfortunate victims of this kind of damage will consistently misreport the past while insisting that they are telling the truth.

Other strikingly extreme demonstrations of confabulation are devised by neuroscientist Michael Gazzaniga. (1970;1985; 1988) Gazzaniga describes a method of eliciting verbal responses from specific hemispheres in the brains of so-called split-brain patients. Split-brain patients, people with a severed corpus callosum (a mass of tissue connecting the two hemispheres of the brain) have very limited, if any, interaction between the two sides of the brain. Gazzaniga designed an experiment that elicited a particular behavior from one hemisphere in isolation from the other. In his experiment, the other hemisphere had access to neither the stimulus that elicited the action nor to the neural processes that gave rise to that action in the opposite hemisphere. However, when the patient (or more specifically the hemisphere not involved in the action) is asked why he or she performed the action, he or she will give reasons for the action that are often quite elaborate but which, for the most part, have nothing to do with the real reasons underlying the performance of the action by the other hemisphere. The hemisphere responding to the questions has no access to the hemisphere that performs the action, and yet it seems compelled to create stories that rationalize the behavior of the organism as a whole.

Confabulation is clearly at work in the split-brain patients, but what about those of us who are not afflicted with a severed corpus callosum? Well, none of us is fully aware of all the mechanisms that underlie our behavior, so to some extent, so perhaps we are all in a somewhat similar situation to the poor confabulating hemisphere. Since a certain degree of confabulation is inevitable, our heterophenomenological investigation will always be a somewhat complicated business. Confabulation is certainly not limited to abnormal brains. Consider, for instance the difficulties faced by juries attempting to determine the veracity of eye-witness testimony. It is a sad reality that what a witness remembers is likely to effected by context and can easily be altered by suggestion and prejudice.

To illustrate what might be going on in the mind of the confabulator, Dennett considers the radically simplified, case of Shakey, a robot built at Stanford in the 1960s. Shakey was designed to wander around a room containing simple objects like a cube, a pyramid etc. It manipulated the objects using a program that converted the signal from a single black and white video camera mounted on top of Shakey's chassis into motor instructions of various kinds for the robot's wheels. Of course, the real Shakey was certainly not qualified to be the subject of Dennett's heterophenomenological investigation; for one thing this robot had no voice and no ability to monitor his own internal activities. However, Dennett imagined the possibility of outfitting Shakey with a bit of linguistic skill and a varying degree of insight into his own actions. The heterophenomenological investigation of this new version of Shakey, "redesigned to include a more sophisticated repertoire of verbal actions, might go like this:

Why did you move the ramp?
SO I COULD ROLL UP ON THE PLATFORM
And why did you want to do that?

74

TO PUSH THE BOX OFF.
And why did you want to do that?
BECAUSE YOU TOLD ME TO

But suppose we then asked Shakey:

How do you tell boxes from pyramids?

What should we design Shakey to 'say' in reply? Here are three possibilities:

> (1) I scan each 10,000-digit-long sequence of 0s and 1s from my camera, looking for certain patterns of sequences, such as... blahblahblah (a very long answer if we let Shakey go into the details).

> (2) I find the light-dark boundaries and draw white lines around them in my mind's eye; then I look at the vertices; if I find a Y vertex for instance, I know I have a box.

> (3) I don't know; some things just look boxy. It just comes to me. It's by intuition. (CE 92-3)

Each of these three options is related to a different degree of self-knowledge. For example, the first option might be equivalent to the kind of self-knowledge that a machine with access to its own design might possess. Dennett comments that in our own case, self-knowledge is more like (3) than (1) or even (2). We know what's happening, more or less, but we don't know what the mechanisms are that underlie what's happening. Each of these options is a report on the state of the system's knowledge of itself and each of the three is true in its way according to Dennett. However, Dennett goes on to offer a more diabolical rigging of his hypothetical robot whereby he talks about what's going on inside himself in entirely spurious ways. He might for instance claim that

> (4) My TV input drives an internal chisel, which hews a three-dimensional shape out of a block mental clay. Then if my homunculus can sit on it, it's a box; if he falls off it's a pyramid." (CE 94)

75

In this case, it's not that Shakey is lying about what is going on inside him, instead he is describing what it is that he 'thinks' is going on when he distinguishes pyramids and boxes. So, turning again to the human subject of our heterophenomenological research, it is quite conceivable that the author of the heterophenomenological text, the volunteer in the experiment, could certainly be mistaken in his descriptions of himself. In Shakey's case, we would know that his description of himself in (4) is completely mistaken, we have access to his insides and to the program that controls his actions.

Obviously, most heterophenomenologists deal with subjects whose internal mechanisms are hidden from us; all we have is the text. However, it could also be argued, as Ryle claimed, that this is also all that the subject himself has access to. It is quite probable that most of us are in almost the same position with respect to our own minds as those who know us well.

Let's examine, once again, what Dennett's method gives us. To begin with the method describes a world, the subject's heterophenomenological world:

> In which there are various *objects* (intentional objects, in the jargon of philosophy), and in which various things happen to these objects. If someone asks: "What are these objects and what are they made of?" The answer might be "Nothing!" (CE 95)

Nevertheless, once we have the portrait in place, we can then turn to the question of what might explain the *existence* of this heterophenomenological world. The theorist's task is to discover whatever it is in the brain that makes subjects produce the narratives that they do. According to Dennett, to make that discovery is, for all intents, to explain the subject's consciousness.

> Whether items thus portrayed exist as real objects in the brain – or in the soul for that matter – is an empirical matter to investigate. If suitable real candidates are uncovered, we can identify them as the long-sought referents of the subject's terms; if not, we will have to explain why it seems to the subjects that these items exist. (CE 98)

The trouble with consciousness, as most of us experience it, is that we hold a basic set of beliefs about consciousness that are extremely difficult to fit with the biological facts. For instance, one of the most

76

fundamental ideas we have about minds is that wherever there is a conscious mind, there is a single, indivisible and continuous *point of view*. We think of the conscious mind as a unified observer that persists, more or less, through time, examining the contents of experience and at least partially directing the motion of the body. One of the most difficult components of Dennett's project involves understanding the role of this Cartesian view of the mind. On the one hand, he must explain why conscious subjects experience the world in the way they do, while, on the other hand, correcting the idea that the Cartesian view of the mind legitimately applies to the brain.

The Cartesian Theatre

Descartes' account of the disembodied subject has served a complicated set of purposes in modern thought. The principal holdover from the Cartesian view of mental life is what Dennett calls the Cartesian Theatre model of mind. This view of mental life tends to characterize conscious experience as a unitary point of view that acts as a kind of disembodied spectator. Our cultural and philosophical heritage has shaped our view of ourselves as spectators on our own experience. Like an audience member, sitting in a darkened theatre, I sit and watch my experiences pass by on the stage in front of me. The Cartesian account of mental life separates us from the body and the world, viewing it on the stage (or screen) of experience.

While we can easily acknowledge the incoherence of substance dualism as a metaphysical doctrine, it has been very difficult for us to give up on the portrayal of the self that accompanied Descartes' dualism. Dennett's criticism of the Cartesian Theatre model is meant to wean philosophers and scientists from the lingering influence of Descartes philosophy. This influence is felt most strongly with respect to views of consciousness and self-knowledge. Since Descartes, most modern philosophers have taken the belief in our own existence as thinking things as the one thing we can hold onto with complete confidence. Without knowing anything whatsoever about the nature of the physical world, including whether we even have a body, we are able to understand a great deal about ourselves, according to Descartes. We can know the mind with certainty, without knowing anything for certain about the body. Obviously the idea that neuroscience might teach us something about the mind would be ruled out by a Cartesian. For Cartesians the mind is already more clearly and distinctly understood than anything we could ever learn about the body.

This kind of assumption is an impediment to anyone interested in explaining the mind in terms of something more basic, or more clearly understood. If we follow Descartes, and ground our reasoning on the idea that the mind is the thing we know with the greatest possible certainty, we have already precluded the possibility that our study of the mind should begin with the natural world rather than with our own self-knowledge.

This Cartesian route is undeniably tempting. Generations of philosophers have taken subjectivity, our experience of ourselves, as the starting point for philosophical inquiry. Since Descartes, most philosophers have worked to understand subjectivity from the inside out so to speak. They begin with what they take the incorrigible evidence of subjective experience to be, and working from there, they attempt to characterize the limits or nature of human subjectivity.

If we accept the basic premise that the brain is the principal organ of mental life, then Dennett thinks it can be shown that the Cartesian Theatre view of mental life must be incorrect. For Dennett, there is no single 'whole me', or self within the brain, serving as the boss responsible for all my words and deeds. Similarly there is no final point or stage in the brain that can be identified as the locus of experience or consciousness. There are convincing biological reasons to doubt whether evolution would provide us with a single screen or viewing room in the brain where all of our perception and experience could come together, nor is there any positive neurophysiological sign of such an organ.

Dennett calls the idea that there is such a location in the brain, 'Cartesian Materialism', "since it's the view you arrive at when you discard Descartes' dualism, but fail to discard the imagery of a central (but material) Theatre where "it all comes together." (CE 107) Following the work of scientists like Marvin Minsky (1985) and others, Dennett points out that the idea of a point of view makes very little sense in the context of the way the brain actually functions. The problem with the idea of an identifiable *point of view* is that we have no way of specifying where the point of view might be. On a larger scale, for example, at a ball game, in a car, or sitting in class, the idea of a person's having a point of view is perfectly legitimate. However, when we close in on the observer, and try to locate the observer's point of view more precisely, as a point *within* the individual, the simple assumptions that work so well on the larger scales begin to break down (CE 103). So, for example,

> If the 'point' of view of the observer must be smeared over a rather large volume in the observer's brain, the observer's own subjective sense of sequence and simultaneity must be determined by something other than "order of arrival," since order of arrival is incompletely defined until the relevant destination is specified. If A beats B to one finish line but B beats A to another, which result fixes subjective sequence in consciousness? (CE 108-109)

Hence, there is no single point in the brain where all information funnels in. However, surely on the path from the initial stimulation of the senses to the production of action, there is some crucial turning point, some moment where the *I* can mediate between perception and action? Dennett's response is to point out that just because the end points – perception and action – are relatively clear, this is "no guarantee that the same distinctions will continue to apply *all the way in* [...] We must stop thinking of the brain as if it had a single such functional summit or central point. This is not an innocuous shortcut; it's a bad habit." (CE, 111) In order to break this bad habit, Dennett offers an alternative image for how consciousness might work.

. *Multiple drafts*

Dennett introduces the multiple drafts model with the claim that all mental activity is accomplished by a "parallel, multitrack process of interpretation and elaboration of sensory inputs" (CE 111). To understand what this means, consider the constant adjustments your brain must make in order for you to read this text, or to navigate safely around the furniture in your room. The motion of heads, bodies and the ever-flitting saccades of the eye cause images to move erratically around the interior surface of the eyeballs. And yet, despite all this motion and variation, most of us manage to see the objects in our visual field as relatively stable phenomena in three dimensions. Vision is an incredibly complicated achievement. Ordinary visual experience is the product of many processes of adjustment and interpretation whereby relatively discontinuous and disorganized impacts on our sensory surfaces are interpreted, revised and enhanced. What we experience are not the impacts on our sensory surfaces, but rather the outcome of countless editorial processes taking place over large fractions of a second. (CE 112)

Most modern theories of perception recognize that our experience is mediated by neural processes that *interpret* information coming from our sensory surfaces. However, Dennett's Multiple Drafts model differs from similar theories by arguing that:

> Feature detections or discriminations *only have to be made once.* That is, once a particular "observation" of some feature has been made, by a specialized, localized part of the brain, the information content thus fixed does not have to be sent somewhere to be rediscriminated by some master discriminator (CE 113)

What Dennett's innovation is meant to show is that the process of picking out some feature of the world in the sensory systems does not lead to the creation of an additional kind of representation that is then conveyed to some central location for viewing by a Cartesian consciousness of some kind: "discrimination does not lead to a representation of the already discriminated feature for the benefit of the audience in the Cartesian Theatre – for there is no Cartesian Theater." (CE 113)

Streams of activity occurring in various parts of the brain pick out various relevant features of the world. These processes of discrimination are subject to continual editing and revision. Because of the distinct locations and times of these processes, there are always going to be 'multiple drafts' of experience undergoing different stages of editing in different parts the brain simultaneously. So, for example, a radically abbreviated version of the account of visual perception that the multiple drafts model can runs something like this. Photosensitive cells on the retina give rise to a series of processes in the visual cortex (via numerous intermediate processes, many of which involve feedforward and feedback processes of their own). Each of these chains of events in the visual cortex gradually yields discriminations of greater and greater specificity. (CE 134) However, the key point that Dennett emphasizes is their separation.

> At different times and different places, various "decisions" or "judgments" are made; more literally, parts of the brain are caused to go into states that discriminate between different features, e.g., first mere onset of stimulus, then location, then shape, later color (in a different pathway), later still (apparent) motion and eventually object recognition. These localized discriminative states transmit effects to other places, contributing to further discriminations and so forth. (CE 134)

So far so good. At this point, Dennett's account is consonant with the lessons of mainstream neuroscience. However, Dennett's multiple drafts theory is meant to go beyond the widely acknowledged fact that perceptual tasks are divided into multiple processing streams in the brain. He is interested in the philosophical implications of recognizing that there is no central point to which these discriminations all travel and that there is nobody to whom they are all finally supplied. Some of these little neural processing events simply die out after a brief flicker, while others leave traces, managing to carve new pathways for future neural events and perhaps influencing the production of verbal reports or other behavior.

Of course, verbal behavior is not necessarily the final destination for neural processes. However, even if a particular discrimination had no effect on verbal behavior, it might increase the readiness of an organism to see other similar features in the near future, or it might encourage processes that are sensitive to related discriminations. So for example, if you see a picture of a dog, you may be more prone to noticing leashes and dog-houses in the near future, or it may be more likely "that you read the word 'bark' as a sound, not a covering for tree trunks" (CE 135). These neural processing events have different fates and can occur in widely separated areas of cortex. Each one is subject to adjustments that produce new discriminations, but revisions in one processing pathway are not necessarily related or even influenced by revisions in another. This is what Dennett calls the *multitrack* component of neural processing.

The key point for Dennett is that, in a very real sense, *these processes manage to think for themselves*, albeit a very simple kind of thinking. The results of each process can be understood as judgments concerning the information that it takes as an input. While we tend to assume that these processes must feed into some final processing station where the brain can assemble the results of many sub-processes for some master discriminator, Dennett's Multiple Drafts model highlights the otiose nature of this imagined final processing stage. If each of these processing stream can perform the kinds of judgments for which it has developed, then there's no need to have some master consciousness along for the ride.

Brains and Computers that Think for Themselves

The idea that each of these neural sub-processes can think for itself is somewhat counterintuitive. Thinking is generally considered the kind of thing that can take place only at the level of the person. Surely, opponents would claim, it is absurd to suggest that a little neural circuit responding only, for example, to horizontal lines is thinking? Well, perhaps it's not so absurd. Clearly, the hypothetical neural circuit in question has a rather limited range of things it can think about, after all, in the case in question, our imaginary circuit can only perform one kind of action – it responds to the presence of certain patterns of signal that tend to be caused by the impact of horizontal patterns of light on the retina. How can we say that this constitutes something like the judgment "there's a horizontal line in front of me" that a normal human adult might produce?

The great mathematician and philosopher Alan Turing (1936, 1950) introduced a way for us to think about computational (or in this case biological or neural) processes thinking for themselves. Turing showed how intelligence could be decomposed into the kinds of tasks that a simple machine could perform. Imagine that you wish to train a new employee in a particular task. For the sake of exposition, let's suppose that it is a mathematical or accounting task. You find that your new employee has an extremely bad memory and no aptitude for mathematics. Therefore you are forced to furnish him with an extremely detailed written recipe for accomplishing the task. Once this is done, he can follow the recipe closely, and accomplishes his assigned task reliably. Turing's brilliant insight is the recognition that given a sufficiently explicit set of instructions you could just give the recipe to a suitable machine and fire the human worker. In such cases we can "eliminate the middleman," as Turing and Dennett would say "and the thinking just happens."

Thanks to Turing and others, certain kinds of thinking are now conducted extremely well by computers. And a computer is, of course, nothing more than a machine that runs long and very explicit recipes (software) to perform tasks that might otherwise have required human time and energy. So, for example, if we need a computer to perform a specific task, say solving an arithmetical problem or monitoring the temperature in an office building, we break that task down into a series of explicit steps. Each of these steps has to be such that a mechanical process can perform the task described. A successful piece of software will have no gaps, it will tell the machine exactly what to do at each step in the process. In this way, the software captures a precise sequence of steps that anyone attempting to accomplish the task in question could follow. However, the crucial point to recognize is that once the computer software is running on your machine, the computer is doing intelligent things without any supervision – for all intents, the thinking just happens. Of course, the engineer who designed the software had to do the hard work of writing all the code, but when that's accomplished, he or she has managed to design a system that can perform intelligently, by itself. In the case of the processes that take place in the brain, the mechanisms that perform the individual perceptual discriminations are like little machines, crafted by natural selection to do their job without supervision or even acknowledgment from an audience in the Cartesian Theatre.

These little machines perform a set of spatially and temporally distinct processes of discrimination. Dennett calls these processes 'content-fixations.' It is important to emphasize that while they are themselves precisely locatable in both space and time, their onsets do *not* mark the onset of consciousness of their content. (See also, Dennett 1992) Instead, these distributed content-discriminations yield, over the course of time, a stream that emerges from the many processes distributed throughout the brain. This stream is subject to continual adjustment and is never fully settled. As a result, there is no final moment or narrative that can be identified with one's consciousness. For a similar model, see William Calvin's (1990) model of consciousness as "scenario-spinning".

What are the Advantages of the Multiple Drafts Model?

The Multiple Drafts model of consciousness is certainly more faithful to what we now know about the neurobiology and neuroanatomy of the brain than the Cartesian Theatre. However, there are also other reasons for accepting Dennett's theory of consciousness. An important test of a new theory is how well it can handle previously unexplained phenomena. One relatively simple, but unexplained set of psychophysical phenomena that can be explained quite naturally from within the Multiple Drafts model are the so-called 'temporal anomalies' of consciousness. In *Consciousness Explained* and elsewhere, Dennett describes how the Multiple Drafts model can resolve fascinating puzzles such as the color *phi* phenomenon, the cutaneous rabbit and Libet's 'backward referral' of sensory experiences. While it isn't possible to review each of these phenomena here, they all share a startling feature in common. In each case, as we shall see, the mind

83

seems to detect a stimulus before the brain could possibly have time to process the stimulus.

The case we will consider concerns the phenomenon of apparent motion. Apparent motion is a familiar and ubiquitous phenomenon in modern life. For instance, movies and television rely on the brain's tendency weave a rapid succession of still images into a single, continuous moving image. Max Wertheimer (1912) conducted the first studies of apparent motion, which he labeled the *phi* phenomenon. Dennett discusses a variation on the simplest case of the phi phenomenon, where two or more small spots separated by less than 4 degrees of visual angle are briefly lit in rapid succession. For the observer, it will appear that a single spot will seem to move back and forth. (CE 114) The phenomenon itself already contains an interesting temporal anomaly insofar as the subject's experience of the moving dot seems to anticipate the final location of the apparently moving spot. This temporal anomaly was brought out even more clearly in an experiment suggested by the philosopher Nelson Goodman. Goodman wondered what subjects would experience if the two small spots were of different colors. First, a red spot lights up, then a green spot lights up in close succession. What we see in such cases is, at least from the perspective of the Cartesian Theatre model, quite amazing.

In these cases, of course, as predicted by the phi phenomenon, we observe apparent motion of the spot. The weird thing is that half way through its course from its starting point to its finishing point the (apparently) moving spot changes color from red to green. Notice that subjects claim to experience the change in color *before* the appearance of the second spot. So, if they see the (apparently moving) spot turn green *before* seeing the color of the second spot, what on earth is the brain doing? Is this a case of clairvoyance? How can we explain the contents of the heterophenomenological world of the subject? In the subject's heterophenomenological world, the color change happens in mid-trajectory. However, he or she must receive the information about which color the second spot would be from somewhere, so how does it happen?

Two obvious Cartesian responses are likely. For a Cartesian, there must be something that happens in the brain before the experience of the spot's motion and its color switch makes it to the finishing line of consciousness. The first approach that might explain what happened from the Cartesian perspective is what Dennett calls the Stalinesque mechanism

In the brain's editing room, located before consciousness, there is a delay, a loop of slack like the tape delay used in broadcasts of live programs, which gives the censors in the control room a few seconds to bleep out obscenities before broadcasting the signal. *In the editing room*, first frame A, of the red spot arrives, and then when the frame B of the green spot, arrives, some interstitial frames (C and D) can be created and then spliced into the film (in the order A,C,D,B) on its way to projection in the theater of consciousness (CE 120)

The alternative "Orwellian" story doesn't rely on a delay, but says instead that what actually happens is that the history of the experience is rewritten by the brain such that a little after the consciousness of the red spot and the green spot

> (with no illusion of apparent motion at all), a revisionist historian of sorts in the brain's memory library receiving station, notices that the unvarnished history in this instance doesn't make enough sense, so he interprets the brute events, red-followed-by-green, by making up a narrative about the intervening passage. (CE 121)

This Orwellian historian will have to work fast enough to preempt any verbal report of our 'original conscious experience' of the two spots appearing in succession without the intervening apparent motion. The record that the Cartesian consciousness relies on to make its verbal report has already been rewritten by the Orwellian historian such that even though the Cartesian consciousness may say and believe that it saw the motion and the color change, that "is really a memory hallucination, not an accurate recollection of your original consciousness." (CE 121) Those who believe in the Cartesian Theater model must choose some version of either the Stalinesque or Orwellian solution to the problem. However, Dennett offers a convincing set of reasons for believing that there is really only a verbal difference between the two theories. Dennett's claim is that there is no way to distinguish between the two solutions either from the perspective of the observer or from the perspective of the neuroscientist.

> The two theories tell exactly the same story except where they place a mythical Great Divide, a point in time (and hence a place in space) whose fine-grained location is

nothing that subjects can help them locate, and whose location is also neutral with regard to all other features of their theories. This is a difference that makes no difference. (CE 125)

Dennett has a number of arguments supporting the verificational indeterminacy of these two options. (See CE 122-126) However, the main flaw inherent in both Orwellian and Stalineque efforts to explain the color phi phenomenon lies in the attempt to account for the apparent sequence of events (the sequence of events in the heterophenomenological world) in terms of some mechanism that constructs the sequence of events for consciousness. Let's reconsider the heterophenomenological world of the subject in the color phi experiment. He or she believes that

A. A red spot lights up
B. It travels a certain distance
C. At a certain point it switches color to green
D. The green spot continues traveling a certain distance
E. The green spot comes to a halt.

Given the conditions of the experiment and barring premonition, the subject's heterophenomenological world is anomalous. How could he or she have known which color the spot would be (C) *before* the appearance of the second spot (E). What the Cartesian overlooks is the possibility that there is no process of "filling-in" actually taking place for consciousness. Now obviously, there is some event in the brain equivalent to the judgment (C) "At a certain point it switches color to green." However, the Multiple Drafts model suggests that there is no reason to assume that (C) occurs *in consciousness* before (D) and (E) In the first place, why should the brain bother to produce the intervening motion and change in color? Couldn't the brain just "conclude that there was intervening motion, and insert that retrospective conclusion into the processing stream? Isn't that enough?" (CE, 128) It is futile, according to Dennett, to attempt to locate the unambiguous sequence of the subject's consciousness, since no such sequence exists. According to the multiple drafts hypothesis, as we have seen, there are numerous drafts of perceptual experience in circulation at any one time. Fixing a time particular time at which the perceptual systems provide their final verdict to consciousness will always be arbitrary.

So, from Dennett's perspective, there could, for example, be a moment in the subjects brain when (A), (B), (C), (D) and (E) are happening all at once in various parts of the brain. This is a pretty strange way of thinking about perception and judgment, but let's ignore the heterophenomenological world for a moment and focus on the order of physical events in the laboratory. This is the third-person portrait of the events in the color phi experiment. It goes without saying that the delay between the times mentioned is very slight.

Time 1: A red spot lights up on the screen in front of the subject

Time 2: Light from the red spot impinges on the subject's retina causing a chain of neural events. We'll call these events (A), since they are equivalent (given a few grains of salt) to the judgment "a red spot lights up"

Time 3: A green spot lights up on the screen in front of the subject not far from where the red spot had been.

Time 4: Light from the green spot impinges on the subject's retina causing a chain of neural events. We'll call these events (E), since they are equivalent (given a few grains of salt) to the judgment "a green spot lights up"

Time 5: Since the brain is always on the lookout for moving objects and rarely looking for flashing dots, it judges that these successive moments indicate that there's an object moving. Incomplete or interrupted views of moving objects are common enough that the visual system will discount a slight gap between two presentations of a moving object and will, for the most part, be biased towards the judgment that there is simply one continuous moving object. The most efficient and reliable judgment in cases of this kind is the judgment we'll call (AE): "The object moved." Now, at the same time, though in a different part of the brain the little neural process that is equivalent to (A) is still humming along, as is the little neural process for (E).

The human brain contains processes that are tuned to discriminate between objects by reference to their color. So, along with all the other processes described above, there will also be a set of processes discriminating between the color of the spots. A little after Time 2 and Time 4, these processes will have judged the first spot red and the second green. Although the timing here is not essential to the matter, we could say that elsewhere in the brain at Time 5 or thereabouts, the previously problematic judgment (C) "The object changed color at some point in mid-trajectory from A to E." takes place.

87

The important point to notice about this judgment is that the time it takes place is not crucially important. Of course, to rule out clairvoyance, it will have to take place at some point after Time 4. However, once it takes place, the judgment (C) can stand, by itself, without being integrated into the heterophenomenological sequence ((A), (B), (C), (D), (E)) presented above. Once the judgment "The object changed color at some point in mid-trajectory from A to E." is made, there is no need for any further reorganization of psychological content to take place. The judgment, including the belief about the time the change happened, is now simply part of the dispositional state of the organism. It doesn't need to travel on to some further point to be recognized by consciousness, it is a discrimination that (wherever or whenever it takes place in the brain) fixes a certain content. That content includes a reference to the time of the color-switch, but just as the content of the sentence "John was born in 1972" has no bearing on when it is uttered, likewise our judgment (C) can stand alone and needn't be reinserted into the psychological sequence of judgments before (D) and (E).

Countless empirical questions about the color phi phenomenon remain unanswered. However, once we adopt the multiple drafts model of consciousness, questions like these are no longer mysterious. Instead, they become manageable biological or computational problems.

Beer, Color and Qualitative Experience

Dennett's explanation of the color phi phenomenon is intended to demonstrate the plausibility of the Multiple Drafts model of consciousness in contrast to the traditional Cartesian Theatre model. However, one aspect of the old view that persists is the notion that subjective experience has properties that cannot be captured by the third-person perspective. The term "qualia" ("qualia" is the plural of "quale") is a piece of philosophical jargon that is meant to capture the distinctively first-person aspects of sensory experiences. According to philosophical orthodoxy, qualia are the subjective feelings that accompany our experiences. They are *what it's like* to perceive, feel, hope, desire etc.

For those who take materialism and information processing models of the mind seriously, qualia seem to pose a major problem. We certainly seem to have something like qualia, and yet if the brain is an information processing machine, as Dennett argues, it is difficult to imagine any real role for consciousness. Each of the processes of content-fixation described previously is an independent little machine, and as such, these processes can perform their function without the kind of conscious accompaniment that we often assume *must* be there. Philosophers have argued that qualitative experience cannot arise from any sort of computational or neural transformation.

Dennett takes aim at the notion of qualia by claiming that "contrary to what seems obvious at first blush, there simply are no qualia at all" (Dennett 1988, 74; also see CE chap. 12, "Qualia Disqualified"). While he agrees that there *seem* to be qualia, he denies the existence of qualia in the kind of contentious, realist sense that many philosophers insist upon. (BC, 141) But surely, philosophers have argued, there is something it is like to see red or to taste the bitterness of a lemon. This something, according to many philosophers eludes scientific description. How could a scientist capture the way a lemon tastes to me in a way that I could share with you?

There seem to be qualia, according to Dennett, because it seems as if science has shown us that things like colors, tastes and smells can't be out there and hence must be in the mind somehow. The seventeenth century philosopher John Locke distinguished between what he called *secondary qualities* (tastes, colors, aromas, tickles, etc.) and *primary qualities* (things like size, length, motion, number etc.). For Locke, primary qualities were the primary objects of scientific inquiry. While secondary qualities were the effects of certain sets of primary qualities on the minds of observers. So the secondary quality of a lemon's bitter taste is the result of the power of a certain primary quality (presumably the shape of the molecules in the lemon juice) on the mind of the lemon taster.

In order to understand the place of these allegedly secondary qualities in science, Dennett examines the nature of color. What science has shown us, according to Dennett, is that the reflective power of objects causes "creatures to go into various discriminative states, scattered about in the brains, and underlying a host of innate dispositions and learned habits of varying complexity." (CE, 372) For Dennett, these discriminative states and the effects they precipitate in the organism are themselves primary qualities. They are purely physical or mechanical states in the brain. However, Dennett remarks "in virtue of these primary properties [the discriminative states] have various secondary, merely dispositional properties. In human creatures with language, for instance, these discriminative states often eventually dispose the creatures to express verbal judgments alluding to the "color" of the thing." (CE, 373) So, in his usual materialist fashion,

Dennett replaces Locke's ideas of red" with discriminative states in normal human beings that have the content: *red.* (CE, 373).

Contrary to the traditional view of color, the function of these discriminative states is *not* to simply pick out certain unique wavelengths of visible light. We have long understood that surfaces with the same reflective capacity can be seen as having different colors under various lighting conditions. Following work described by Gouras, (1984) Hilbert (1987) and Hardin (1988) Dennett recognizes that the perception of color is primarily a matter of making comparisons between objects rather than picking out unique wavelengths of light. The discriminative mechanisms in the brain have evolved to pick out and compare objects by reference to the relative degrees to which they reflect certain portions of the visible spectrum among all the other objects in the visual field. Contrary to Locke's hope, since our color judgments do not picking out unique wavelengths of light, we cannot infer that the dispositional powers of certain sets of primary qualities in surfaces are the principal source of our perception of color.

As with so many aspects of mental life, Dennett turns again to Darwin, for an explanation of color perception. Consider color vision in insects. The principles of natural selection would seem to show that insect color vision co-evolved with the colors of the plants they pollinated. "A good trick of design that benefited both. Without the color-coding of the flowers, the color vision of the insects would not have evolved, and vice versa." (CE, 377) Dennett's explanation of color-vision is strikingly simple: "Some things in nature "needed to be seen" and others needed to see them, so a system evolved that tended to minimize the task for the latter by heightening the salience of the former. " (CE, 377)

If this is an accurate account of the co-evolutionary origin of color vision then it seems as though judgments about color are dependent on the class of entities making the judgment. However, surely we can claim that a flower that would normally appear to have the color X to a bumblebee would still have that property even if no insect had ever seen the flower. Perhaps, but the important point to notice is that the property "having the color X" in this plant is fixed primarily by reference to the visual discriminations performed by a specific audience of bumblebees. Since we have an account of the co-evolution of these discriminative capacities, natural selection prevents our falling into the kind of "subjectivism" or "relativism" implied by the idea that secondary qualities depend on the observer.

Evolutionary explanations help to account for some of the reasons that secondary qualities seem so difficult to explain. There is no simple property that can be identified with the kinds of qualitative experiences that we find so fascinating because they almost always arise in out of our relationship with certain important parts of our environment. Our sensory systems are tuned to pick out those things in the natural world that can either benefit us or do us harm. So, in a sense, secondary qualities are inevitably matters of comparison rather than occasions where we manage to pick out the essence of something in the natural world.

> It shows that the absence of "simple" or "fundamental" commonalities in things that are the same color is not an earmark of total illusion, but rather, is a sign of widespread tolerance for false positive detections of the ecological properties that really matter. (CE381)

In addition to his analysis of the co-evolution of secondary qualities, Dennett's argument against the existence of qualia rests on his denial of Cartesian Materialism. According to Dennett, the traditional arguments for qualia are predicated on the idea that there is a central Cartesian subject, for whom experience has qualities of one kind or another. Once we give up this belief, he suggests, the grip of the idea of qualia as private atoms of personal experience is loosened considerably. Such arguments may still leave the lovers of qualia unconvinced. We all know, they argue, that tastes, flavors, aromas, colors and all the rest, have a distinctive and powerful reality, no matter what arguments Dennett presents.

According to Dennett, our knowledge of qualia is less certain than the qualiaphile would admit. In fact, it is difficult to do much more with the philosophical concept of qualia than to insist on their importance and express our confidence in their existence. When we try to fix on something definite that a quale could be, we run into the same kinds of indeterminacy arguments that Dennett had previously brought to bear against the Stalinesque and Orwellian interpretations of the color phi phenomenon. So, for example, in 'Quining Qualia,' (1988) Dennett imagines a coffee-taster who, after six years at the company, is unsure of whether he still tastes coffee the same way he did when he joined the company. The coffee-taster wonders whether his taste qualia, his memory, or his standards of judgments have changed over the years. The coffee, presumably, is chemically identical over the years, so something about his sensory apparatus must have changed over time. Dennett argues that there is a fundamental verificational indeterminacy among these (ostensibly) competing hypotheses, at least from the perspective of the coffee-taster's heterophenomenology. If anything is going to answer his questions about qualia it will have to come from somewhere other than his phenomenology. So, for instance, many of us enjoy the taste of beer. However, for almost everybody, the first taste of beer is not an especially pleasant experience. We come to enjoy the taste of beer over time and yet, Dennett wonders, what precisely is the taste that we are now enjoying? The heterophenomenological difference between our first beer and our thousandth is clear, but what can we say has changed between beer number one and beer number one thousand. The two alternatives that the lover of qualia will propose are either:

(A) The way beer tastes to us gradually changes
(B) It's the same taste, but drinkers gradually come to enjoy the taste that formerly nauseated them.

In order for qualia talk to be coherent, one of these choices must be true. And in order to determine which is true, it will be necessary to go behind the heterophenomenology to the "actual happenings in the head to see whether there is a truth-preserving (if "strained") interpretation of the beer drinkers' claims." (CE, 396) However, if there is something in the head that makes either A or B true, it will only be because we have decided to identify "the way beer tastes" with some set of neural processes or another. (See also Dennett, 1988) So, Dennett concludes given the phenomenological indeterminacy that inevitably arises in such cases, "[w]e would have to "destroy" qualia in order to "save" them." (CE, 396) Hence, the existence of qualia, at least in the mysterious sense seems to have been disproved.

A complete presentation of Dennett's mature theory of consciousness can be found in his brazenly titled book *Consciousness Explained* (1991). Though Dennett had already presented a theory of the relationship between language and consciousness as early as his *Content and Consciousness* (1969), the present chapter has focused on his published work from 1978 to the present. One of the most significant differences between this second period and the account he gave in *Content and Consciousness* is his emphasis in the later work on the role of neuroscience and cognitive psychology in the explanation of the subpersonal mechanisms that support consciousness. Writing in 1985, in the preface to the second edition of his first book, Dennett points out some of the 'dramatic shortcomings' of the early account of consciousness. Little, if anything, from Part II of *Content and Consciousness* is retained in his mature work. This is evidence of his diminished confidence in the techniques of the ordinary language philosophers and his increasingly scientific orientation with respect to the problem of consciousness.

As we have seen, for most of the twentieth century consciousness was considered an intractably mysterious phenomenon; something neither science nor philosophy could hope to grasp in any meaningful way. Many philosophers believed that the notion of consciousness was lacking in any genuine scientific content. Similarly, as we saw in Chapter Two, psychologists in the behaviorist tradition famously argued that the very idea of an inner life is a metaphysical illusion. Behaviorists, it has been charged, "feign anesthesia" denying that they, or anyone else, is really conscious. When Dennett began working on the problem, philosophical and scientific prejudices against the study of consciousness were still quite strong. However, times have changed, and in recent years a huge academic industry has sprung up around the topic. Consciousness, it seems, is once again a respectable topic of scientific conversation. Dennett is correctly viewed as one of the people who laid the groundwork for recent scientific and philosophical investigations of consciousness.

One remarkable aspect of Dennett's work is the way he reframes traditional problems so as to bring the lessons of our best science and philosophy into dialogue with one another. This ability to reframe traditional problems will ensure Dennett's place in the history of philosophy. Dennett will be known as the philosopher who broke "the spell of the enchanted circle of ideas that made explaining consciousness seem impossible." (CE 455)

Concluding Remarks

The principal task of this short book has been to introduce readers to Dennett's philosophy of mind. As such, this has been an incomplete introduction to Dennett's work. Among the important topics that I have not addressed include Dennett's views on ethics. For those views, I urge interested readers to begin with his book *Elbow Room: Varieties of Free Will Worth Wanting* as well as Chapter Sixteen and Seventeen of his *Darwin's Dangerous Idea: Evolution and the Meanings of Life*. It goes without saying that fields like molecular biology, evolutionary biology and neuroscience hold important implications for ethical theory. If we wish to understand what science and contemporary philosophy can tell us about our lives, Dennett is one of the most uncompromising guides in the business.

Dennett has described his philosophy as an attempt to "[work] out some of the surprising implications of the standard scientific picture." This picture doesn't require that we know all the details of our latest and best physics. Instead, it simply requires what he calls "a normal respect for science –*Time Magazine* standard, nothing more doctrinaire" (DAC, 205). However, a significant number of commentators, from postmodern critics of scientific objectivity to religious fundamentalists of various kinds, have opposed science, seeing it as a dangerous threat to our humanity. This perceived threat is accompanied by a tendency in certain quarters to resist any encroachment of science on matters pertaining to the human mind. They worry about the effects of science on our moral, aesthetic or political lives. For these thinkers, an empirically-minded philosopher like Dennett is "something of a villain: a science-crazed, insensitive mechanist, with a bleak and inhuman world-view" (DAC, 9).

According to some conservatives and many romantics, the scientific worldview has demystified and thereby devalued human life and the natural world. This inference is unwarranted. While science may have destroyed any basis for the belief in a "spirit" understood as some kind of "essential self" that exists apart from human biology, this is only because a view of human nature that depends the existence of a disembodied self is almost certainly false. It is a mistake to infer that that human life or the natural world is meaningless simply because we have no reason to believe in supernatural forces, disembodied souls, fundamentalist creation myths etc. Dennett's work provides a way for us to reconcile ordinary psychological and ethical judgments with the lessons of natural science, helping us to understand these puzzling phenomena without relying on supernatural objects or forces.

BIBLIOGRAPHY:

Bickle, J. (1998) *Psychoneural reduction: the new wave.* Cambridge
 MA: MIT Press.
Brentano, F. (1995) [1874] (*T Crane and J. Wolff* eds. A.C. Rancurello,
 D.B. Terrell and L. McAlister trans.) *Psychology from an
 Empirical Standpoint.* London: Routledge. Originally
 published as *Psychologie vom empirischen Standpunkte*
 Leipzig: Duncker & Humblot.
Calvin, W. (1990) *The Cerebral Symphony: Seashore Reflections on
 the Structure of Consciousness.* New York: Bantam.
Chisholm, R. (1957). *Perceiving: A Philosophical Study.* Ithaca:
 Cornell University Press.
Chisholm, R. (1966). 'On some Psychological Concepts and the 'Logic
 of Intentionality' in H.N. Castaneda, ed *Intentionality, Minds
 and Perception.* Detroit: Wayne State University Press.
Churchland, P.M. (1981) 'Eliminative Materialism and the
 Propositional Attitudes.' *Journal of Philosophy,* 78, 67-90.
Dahlbom, B. (ed.) (1993) *Dennett and his Critics,* Oxford: Blackwell.
Dennett, Daniel C. (1969) *Content and Consciousness.* International
 Library of Philosophy and Scientific Method. New York:
 Humanities Press; London: Routledge & Kegan Paul.
Dennett, Daniel C. (1978) *Brainstorms: Philosophical Essays on Mind
 and Psychology.* Montgomery, Vt.: Bradford Books.
Dennett, Daniel C. (1981) 'Three Kinds of Intentional Psychology.' In
 R. Healy, ed., Reduction, Time and Reality (Cambridge:
 Cambridge University Press) 37-61
Dennett, Daniel C. (1982) 'How To Study Human Consciousness
 Empirically, or Nothing Comes to Mind,' *Synthese,* 59, 159-
 180.
Dennett, Daniel C. (1984) *Elbow Room: The Varieties of Free Will
 Worth Wanting.* Cambridge, Mass.: MIT Press.
Dennett, Daniel C. (1987) *The Intentional Stance.* Cambridge, Mass.:
 MIT Press.
Dennett, Daniel C. (1988a) 'Quining Qualia.' In: A. Marcel and
 Bisiach, E., *Consciousness and Contemporary Science.* New
 York: Oxford University Press.
Dennett, Daniel C. (1988b) 'Précis of *The Intentional Stance*' in Brain
 and Behavioral Sciences **11,** 495-546
Dennett, Daniel C. (1991) *Consciousness Explained.* Boston: Little,
 Brown.

Dennett, Daniel C. (1992) 'Temporal anomalies of consciousness: implications of the uncentered brain.' In: Y. Christen and P. S. Churchland (eds.) *Neurophilosophy and Alzheimer's Disease*. Berlin: Springer-Verlag.

Dennett, Daniel C. (1995) *Darwin's Dangerous Idea: Evolution and the Meanings of Life*. New York: Simon and Schuster; London: Allen Lane.

Dennett, Daniel C. (1995) 'The Unimagined Preposterousness of Zombies," *Journal Of Consciousness Studies*, 2 322-36.

Dennett, Daniel C. (1996) *Kinds of Minds: Toward an Understanding of Consciousness*. (The Science Masters Series.) New York: Basic Books.

Dennett, Daniel C. (1998) *Brainchildren: Essays on Designing Minds*. Cambridge, Mass.: MIT Press, A Bradford Book,

Dennett, Daniel C. (1999) 'The Zombic Hunch: Extinction of an Intuition?' Royal Institute of Philosophy Millennial Lecture.

Fodor, J. (1975), *The Language of Thought*. Hassocks, Sussex: Harvester Press.

Fodor, J. and E. Lepore (1993) "Is Intentional Ascription Intrinsically Normative." In B. Dahlbom ed. *Dennett and his Critics*. Cambridge MA: Blackwell.

Gazzaniga, M. (1988) *Mind Matters: How the Mind & Brain Interact to Create Our Conscious Lives*. Boston: Houghton.

Gazzaniga, M. (1985) *The Social Brain: Discovering the Networks of Mind*. New York: Basic Books.

Gazzaniga, M. (1970) *The Bisected Brain*. New York: Appleton-Century-Crofts. .

Gouras, P. (1984) "Color Vision, " in N. Osborn and J. Chader, eds., *Progress in Retinal Research*. Vol 3 London: Pergamon Press.

Grandy, R. (1973) "Reference, Meaning and Belief," *Journal of Philosophy,* 70, 439-52

Hardin, C.L. (1988) *Color For Philosophers: Unweaving the Rainbow*. Indianapolis; Hackett.

Hilbert, D.R. (1987) *Color and Color Perception: A Study in Anthropocentric Realism*; Center for the Study of Language and Information, Stanford.

Hooker, C.A (1981) "Towards a General Theory of Reduction. Part I: Historical and Scientific Setting. Part II: Identity in Reduction. Part III: Cross Categorical Reduction" *Dialogue* 20: 38-59, 201-236, 496-529.

Lewis, C.S (1960). *Studies in Words,* Oxford: Oxford University Press.

McGinn, C. (1995) "Consciousness Evaded: Comments on Dennett." In

James E. Tomberlin, ed., *AI, Connectionism and Philosophical Psychology. Philosophical Perspectives, 9.* Ridgeview: Atascadero.

Minsky, M. (1985) *The Society of Mind.* New York: Simon Schuster

Nagel, E. (1961) *The Structure of Science.* New York: Harcourt Brace and World.

Nagel, T. (1974) "What is it like to be a bat?" *Philosophical Review* 83, 435-450.

Nagel, T. (1995) *Other Minds: Critical Essays 1969-1994.* New York & Oxford: Oxford University Press, Especially, chapter 7 "Dennett: Content and Consciousness" and chapter 8 "Dennett: Consciousness Dissolved."

Nozick, R. (1981) *Philosophical Explanations.* Cambridge, MA: Harvard University Press.

Place, U.T. (1956) "Is Consciousness a Brain Process?" *British Journal of Psychology* 47, 44-50.

Putnam, H. "Why there isn't a Ready Made World" *Synthese* (1982 51 141-167)

Quine, W.V.O. (1960) *Word and Object,* Cambridge, MA: MIT Press.

Quine, W.V.O. (1969) 'Epistemology Naturalized' in *Ontological Relativity and Other Essays,* New York: Columbia University Press

Ryle, G. (1949) *The Concept of Mind,* London: Hutchinson's.

Stich, S. (1996) *Deconstructing the Mind* Oxford: Oxford University Press.

Stich, S. and I. Ravenscroft 'What *is* Folk Psychology' in Stich (1996)

Tolman, E.C. (1948) 'Cognitive Maps in Rats and Men' *Psychological Review* 55:189-208

Turing, A. (1950) "Computing Machinery and Intelligence," Mind, 59 433-460

Turing, A. (1936) "On Computable Numbers, with an Application to the *Entscheidungs-Problem*" *Proceedings of the London Mathematical Society,* Series 2, 42:230-265

Tye, M. (1993) "Reflections on Dennett and Consciousness." *Philosophy and Phenomenological Research* 53(4):893-898.

Watson, J.B. (1925) [1913] *Behaviorism.* New York: Norton.

Wertheimer, M. (1912) "Experimentelle Studien über das Sehen von Bewegung," *Zeitschrift für Psychologie,* 61 161-265.

Yu, P. and Fuller, G. (1986) "A Critique of Dennett." *Synthese* 66(3):453-476.